OTHER TITLES FROM BLACK BEACON BOOKS

Novels by Cameron Trost:

Letterbox
The Tunnel Runner

Collections by Cameron Trost:

The Animal Inside
Hoffman's Creeper and Other Disturbing Tales

Anthologies:

Murder and Machinery
The Black Beacon Book of Mystery
Shelter from the Storm
Lighthouses
Subtropical Suspense

blackbeaconbooks.com

Oscar TREMONT

Investigator of the Strange and Inexplicable

Cameron TROST

Oscar Tremont, Investigator of the Strange and Inexplicable
by Cameron Trost

Published by Black Beacon Books
Cover design by Cameron Trost
Copyright © Black Beacon Books, 2022

All rights reserved. No part of this publication may be reproduced or transmitted by any means without the prior permission of the author.

Thank you for respecting the author's work.

Black Beacon Books
www.blackbeaconbooks.com

ISBN: 978-0-9923211-5-4

Cameron Trost is an author of mystery and suspense fiction. *Oscar Tremont, Investigator of the Strange and Inexplicable* is his first collection of puzzles featuring his intrepid private detective. He has written two novels, *Letterbox* and *The Tunnel Runner*, and two other collections, *Hoffman's Creeper and Other Disturbing Tales* and *The Animal Inside*. He runs the independent press, Black Beacon Books, and is a lifetime member of the Australian Crime Writers Association. Originally from Brisbane, Australia, Cameron lives with his wife and two sons near Guérande in southern Brittany, between the rugged coast and treacherous marshlands.

camerontrost.com

The Hunt for the Stayne Fortune…7

The Ghosts of Walhalla…78

The Witch at the Window…171

The Secret of the Severed Hand…209

The Hunt for the Stayne Fortune

1.

Archives Fine Books was a place of mystery and enchantment. The sign attached to the building's red brick façade boasted that one million books could be found within its venerable walls, and Oscar Tremont, Investigator of the Strange and Inexplicable, wasn't inclined to challenge that claim. He often lost himself in the shop's maze of dusty aisles. Many of the rare books that occupied the simple wooden shelves of that grand old building dated from the early nineteenth century. Some were even older than the city of Brisbane itself.

Oscar studied the scribbles that decorated the title page of the book he'd just removed from the local history shelf. He knew what he'd stumbled across was more than just a mere side note. The message wasn't in English—that was obvious enough—and Oscar's linguistic skills enabled him to deduce that it didn't belong to any other language that used the Roman alphabet.

There was only one logical conclusion. It was some kind of code.

His work found him investigating all kinds of obscure matters, from seemingly impossible thefts and suspected cases of stalking to ghostly apparitions and strange nocturnal happenings. But, much to his regret, no client had ever asked him to crack a code.

He stroked his moustache and drew a deep breath—the distinct smell of aged paper was almost as soothing to him as the smoky bouquet of a dram of Lagavulin. He then focused on the words jotted down on the title page of the book in his hands—a nineteenth-century edition of John Oxley's *Journals of Two Expeditions into the Interior of New South Wales.*

His rudimentary knowledge in the field of cryptology wasn't going to be sufficient to make cracking this particular code an easy task. Whoever had written the message had used a code he'd never come across before. His curiosity was well and truly piqued, and for Oscar Tremont, curiosity was just a step away from the steely grip of obsession.

He looked up and down the gloomy aisle of the bookshop. A young woman was scanning a row of books just above her eye level. She must have been a few years younger than Oscar, perhaps in her late twenties. She was pretty, with shoulder-length brown hair and pale skin that looked like porcelain. She had a piercing through her bottom lip—a cone-shaped stud that moved in and out as her face changed from one expression to another while she browsed. Her head was cocked to one side so that she could read the spines of the books in front of her and her glasses were balanced perilously on her nose. She was hypnotised and didn't seem to notice Oscar at all. He was all too familiar with that feeling himself.

Another bookworm was tunnelling his way along a nearby shelf. Oscar could hear a man's footsteps on the wooden floor. They were coming from the aisle parallel to where he stood. Somebody wearing hiking shoes—the kind he'd noticed were favoured by Scandinavian backpackers—was browsing the travel guides section.

As far as he could tell, the only other people in the shop,

apart from the girl at the register, were the characters that dwelt within the pages of the innumerable books surrounding him.

Satisfied that nobody realised what he'd discovered, and with his paranoia now placated, Oscar turned his attention back to the code. The book had been published in the late nineteenth century, but the code could have been written at just about any time between then and now. As he stared at the text, he barely noticed the young woman squeezing past behind him, as quiet as a mouse.

Eventually, he looked up and shook his head. The strange words meant nothing to him.

He would have to do a spot of research. He walked the passages of the vast bookshop, the wooden floor creaking under his black Doc Martens. He skipped the sections that had nothing to do with codes and slowly inspected those that might have some relevance, like military non-fiction and languages.

But it was all in vain. He failed to find even a single title that shed any light on the matter.

The backpacker appeared from around a corner and walked back towards the counter with an old and presumably out-of-date travel guide to Australia. He obviously didn't mind trying to book nights at hostels that were no longer in business.

Oscar decided the internet would be his best bet. He could try entering the words of the code into a search engine in order to see if there'd be a translation in the results. It would amount to cheating, but without a key to the code, he didn't have much choice. He'd do that at home on his laptop, after making a pot of herbal tea.

There was just one problem. He looked at the price, written in pencil on the inside cover of the book, and bit his bottom lip. As much as he wanted to crack the code—no, not wanted, he reminded himself, *had to* crack it—he couldn't justify spending eighty dollars on a book.

He walked back to the local history section and found the gap where the book had been, took his phone from his jacket and took a picture of the code, then closed the book and put it back on the shelf.

'See you soon,' the girl at the counter said. He went to *Archives* often enough that she recognised him. Perhaps she even considered him a regular.

'Have a good day,' he replied.

It was still sunny but not especially hot outside. He flipped his handmade Irish flat cap onto his shaved head and put his pair of round sunglasses on. He then pulled the chain attached to his belt and consulted his pocket watch. It was a short train ride from the city centre to his small cottage in Wilston, but he wasn't in a hurry so decided to walk instead. Exercise helped him think.

2.

Oscar stared at his kettle as though it might hold the answer. When the water came to a boil, he poured it into his teapot and watched as the dried herbs somersaulted and pirouetted in the white china strainer. He closed his eyes for a moment and inhaled deeply, drawing the tendrils of steam into his nostrils and letting the fragrance fill his mind. After a while, he opened his eyes and carried the teapot and a cup out to the verandah, where his laptop was waiting for him on an antique tea trolley. Once he'd placed the teapot and cup on the trolley, he took the laptop and sat on his deck chair, which Louise had dubbed his *thinking chair*—even though her French accent made it sound like a financial investment error.

In any case, he certainly had plenty of thinking to do.

An image search for *secret codes* resulted in a plethora of pictures for Pigpen, Templar, and cattle earmark codes, as well as the classics, like the Caesar and Beaufort ciphers. He began applying the relevant forms of code to the scribbling from the book. But he gave up on trawling the net when he'd emptied the teapot. There was little doubt the code was an original one. Somebody had dreamed it up. He felt a peculiar mix of frustration and relief. He'd wanted a challenge, and he'd certainly got one.

He went back to the kitchen to boil some more water. Louise would be home from work in a couple of hours and he wanted to have the puzzle sorted out and his mind put at ease before then.

Assuming the code was just a substitution code, the next step would be to go through the entire alphabet, substituting each letter for another until a word was revealed. He was thankful there were spaces between the words. That would make the task a great deal easier. Again, assuming that one code letter represented one regular letter, the first word was three letters long. He would follow the premise that this first word was *the* and try to break the code accordingly.

Oscar poured hot water into his teapot and returned to his thinking chair. He looked at the code again:

Dvy Cdojpy zoqurj znbdfpy uc xfurd np o znfpeodunp nz xydbojor ope cup. Hy qfcd lnqy dnwydvyb dn mfd buwvd orr dvy hbnpw dvod voc xyyp enpy. Dvy zoqurj spnhc dvod u vogy mbnnz nz udc ygur eyyec ope uc hodlvupw qy. Mowy dhypdj-zugy vnrec dvy syj. 5 ope 9 uc 1 ope 2, dvy rocd 4 lnqy rocd.

After replacing every *d* with the letter *t*, *v* with an *h*, and *y* with an *e*, he had a text that looked a little clearer. He also decided to work on the assumption that the solitary letters *o* and *u* were probably *a* and *I*, but there was no way of knowing which was which.

He sipped his tea and let its soothing warmth spread through his body, then closed his eyes and listened to the few sounds that reached his ears. Wilston was a quiet family suburb, especially during the day while parents were at work and children were at the city's most prestigious schools. Oscar and his wife rented a small yet comfortable cottage that was undoubtedly the most unassuming house on Dover Street. They didn't have any children yet, but they wanted a family and knew the clock was ticking. What worried him, though, was the knowledge that raising a family would require a steadier income than the one he was currently bringing in. In a city like Brisbane, both parents had to be on a decent wage just to stay afloat. Louise had a stable position in a company exporting agricultural machinery to New Caledonia. Would Oscar have to change his line of work—stop the freelance detective gig? It was a disturbing prospect. He couldn't imagine working in an office with colleagues. That would drive him mad. More precisely, he'd drive *them* mad.

The cawing of crows reminded Oscar that he wasn't completely alone in the world. They cried out across the sky from the tops of the handful of Norfolk pines that encircled Wilston. There was also the faint but constant drone of traffic coming from Newmarket Road.

Then there was another sound that disturbed the quiet—approaching footsteps. Oscar, his eyes still closed, took a deep breath and held it so he could hear more clearly. The footsteps were those of a man. They fell silent as they stepped from the road to the stretch of grass that lay before the gate to the narrow front garden. He heard the old double swing gate being pulled open. It creaked noisily. Boot soles sounded against four brick steps—one at a time.

'Edgar, how are you, mate?'

The footsteps stopped in their tracks.

'When are you going to tell me how you do that?'

'You know very well that I'm waiting for *you* to tell *me* how I do it.'

It was quite simple in fact. Edgar had the unusual habit of pulling the gate open whereas most people pushed it inwards. The gate made a different creaking sound depending on which way it was opened. Also, quite naturally, he recognised his friend's footsteps, especially when he was wearing his R.M. Williams boots. Then there was the fact that Edgar didn't hesitate at the top of the stairs, which indicated he was someone who felt at ease entering the property—not a stranger. Lastly, while most men tended to descend the steps two at a time, Edgar had the habit of taking one step at a time.

It was just a matter of simple observation.

'Are you working on a case?'

Oscar opened his eyes and frowned.

'I'm afraid not. There seems to be a lull in the strange and inexplicable at the moment. Tedium is the order of the day. However, I came across something of interest at *Archives* this morning.'

Edgar sat on a deck chair. 'That's no surprise.'

'Yes, but this is *really* interesting. I stumbled across a coded message.'

Edgar sat upright and raised his eyebrows. He wondered for an instant whether Oscar was pulling his leg, but he quickly realised he was serious.

'What kind of code is it?'

'That's what I've been trying to work out. I'm beginning to suspect it's a keyword cipher.'

'Do you have any idea what the keyword could be?'

'Not yet, but that's my next angle of attack.'

'You found the code in a book?'

'In a copy of John Oxley's *Journals of Two Expeditions into the Interior of New South Wales*. Do you have time to help me go through some likely keywords, Edgar? Your lot are good at that sort of thing.'

'My lot—the IT crowd?' He laughed. 'Well, I suppose we are, and of course I have time for my best mate.'

'Excellent. You know how a keyword cipher works, don't you?'

'I think so. The first letters of the alphabet are replaced with the letters making up a keyword and then the subsequent letters are replaced with the remaining letters of the alphabet.'

Oscar nodded as he turned his laptop so Edgar could see the screen. 'That's the general idea, but it's not always that simple.'

'Let's make a list of possible keywords,' Edgar suggested.

'You mean *probable* keywords.'

He smiled. 'Yes, of course. Probable ones.'

'Well, we have the book I found the code in. Likely keywords include the author and title; *John*, *Oxley*, and *journals*.'

Edgar nodded. 'As well as the words *expeditions* and *interior*.'

Oscar shook his head and frowned. 'I disagree there. Both words have repeated letters. *Expeditions* has the letter *e* twice and the letter *i* twice. *Interior* has *i* and *r* twice. I think we should start by looking at words that don't have doubles of any letters.'

'Fair point. That makes more sense,' Edgar admitted. 'Can you send me an email with the code so I can play around with it on my phone?'

'It's on its way. Do you want a cup of coffee?'

'Yes, please. I'll get started by trying *John* as a keyword.'

They worked through the keywords quickly, ruling them out one by one. Oscar's initial idea of treating the first three letter word, *dvy,* as *the* didn't fit in with any of the keywords they'd identified as likely. With *John* as keyword, *d* would represent *h*, not *t*, and with *Oxley* as keyword, it would represent *i*. The results were the same for every other keyword they tested. Oscar decided to abandon the idea of assuming that the first word was *the*, but he couldn't find any words beginning with *h* or *i* that could be used to start a text and matched the keywords he'd thought up. *His*, *her*, *how*, and *had* just didn't fit. Neither did *its* and *ice*. Nothing seemed to make any sense.

'I'm going to try using the alphabet in reverse,' Oscar announced with a sigh once he'd exhausted every keyword on his list and finished his tea.

'You mean, for example, using *John* as a keyword for *abcd* and then *zyxw* and so forth for *efgi* onwards?'

'Exactly.'

Edgar groaned. 'This thing's really got you hooked, hasn't it?'

'You know it has,' Oscar said, shaking his head. 'The harder it gets, the more I want to crack it, and preferably before Louise gets home and distracts me.'

'Distracts you by telling you to get a real case with a client who's alive today and in a position to pay, you mean?'

'That's precisely what I mean.'

Oscar kept at it, now applying the same keywords to the alphabet in reverse. Once he'd started using *Oxley*, a handful of short words started to appear out of the jumble of nonsense. *Ope* became *and*, *nz* morphed into *of*, *qy* revealed itself as *me*, and *np* transformed itself into *on*. On the other hand, the words with two letters *dn* and *uc* made *wo* and *ix* respectively.

'I'm getting there, Edgar! There's still a glitch, but I'm definitely getting closer. You need to use *Oxley* as the keyword followed by the remaining letters of the alphabet in reverse order.'

'All right, I'm onto it.'

After several minutes working on the code, they both came up with an identical version of the text:

Whe Xwarne familr foywvne ix bvilw on a fovndawion of bewyaral and xin. Te mvxw come wogewhey wo pvw yighw all whe tyong whaw hax been done. Whe familr knotx whaw I haue pyoof of iwx euil deedx and ix tawching me. Page wtenwr-fiue holdx whe ker. 5 and 9 ix 1 and 2, whe laxw 4 come laxw.

'We're close!' Edgar announced, rubbing his hands together. 'We can almost work out what it says!'

'I know what it says, my friend. I'm glad we didn't give up. Now, we need to get back to *Archives* before it closes.' He consulted his pocket watch. 'You didn't drive here, did you? No, of course not. You walked from the station. Never mind. We'll take my car. I need you to drive me to Charlotte Street.'

Edgar was speechless. He looked at the text again. He could make out a few words; *page* was clear enough, and *family*, *foundation*, and *proof* weren't hard to guess, but he hadn't worked out the entire text yet.

Then, as though a light bulb had come on and chased the darkness away, he understood.

'The alphabet isn't simply in reverse,' he ventured. 'It's split in two after the keyword, *Oxley*. That's it, isn't it?'

'Spot on!' Oscar congratulated him as he leaped to his feet. 'The first part runs from *z* to *m* and the second from *a* to *k*. Come on! Let's go!'

3.

No sooner had Oscar stepped back inside the otherworldly realm of *Archives Fine Books* than the girl greeted him for the second time that day. She didn't seem all that surprised. There was no reason why she should have been. Bookworms often returned after comparing prices and available titles in different shops around town.

'Hello again.'

'Hello, I'm not too late, am I?'

'We're closing in ten minutes.'

'No problem. I know exactly what I'm looking for.' He dashed around to where the book had been, hoping it was still there. There was nobody else in the shop as far as he could tell, although there could have been other customers lurking around in parallel aisles. He felt like he was in a world of his own, out of view of the counter.

The book was still there, naturally enough; who was going to buy an eighty dollar edition of a book that could be downloaded for free from a number of government websites?

Oscar pulled the book from the shelf and looked at the title page again. He read the coded message, mentally replacing the substituted letters with the original ones as he did so. In hindsight, it was so very easy. That was what codes were all about—making the simple seem indecipherable.

He took a pen and scrap of paper from his jacket pocket,

turned to page twenty-five, and was relieved to find that he didn't have to take a photograph of the page or—even worse—fork out eighty dollars to buy the book. The key sentence was underlined with ink that appeared to be identical to that used to write the coded message. All he had to do was make sense of it:

"The means which his Excellency placed at my disposal were well calculated to attain…"

#

Peak hour traffic made the drive back to Wilston a slow one, but Oscar didn't mind. He took advantage of the time to consider how the last sentence of the coded message could help him unlock the key to the mystery he'd stumbled across. His head turned back and forth from the photo on his mobile phone to the sentence scribbled on the back of an Aldi receipt.

Edgar came to a stop at a red light next to the Treasury Casino, a neo-Italianate marvel whose existence, from being a colonial treasury to a fashionable centre of gambling and dining, had long been dedicated to relieving Brisbane residents of their excess cash. Oscar looked at the building briefly, as though expecting the intricacies of John James Clark's architecture to reveal the secrets of the code to him, but the light turned green and Edgar drove on, continuing along George Street.

'I hope this code is worth all the effort we're putting into it,' Edgar remarked.

'So do I,' Oscar agreed.

He lifted his gaze from the mysterious sentence and sighed. They were drawing to a halt at yet another red light. The woman in the car next to them was swinging her shoulders from side to side and singing, although her words were inaudible, trapped within the closed windows of her car. She was happy to be on her way home after a day at the office.

'Promise me something, Edgar.'

'Yes?' he asked suspiciously. He was familiar with Oscar's requests. The last time he'd been asked to make a promise, it had involved meeting up in the wardrobe of an abandoned house at one o'clock in the morning to solve the mystery of a suburban cult suspected of kidnapping pet dogs and cats and— but Edgar didn't want to think about that again. 'Is this the same kind of promise as last time?'

'Last time?'

'Yes—last time. About three months ago. You haven't forgotten the cult already?'

Oscar grinned. 'Oh yes, I made you promise to meet me in the squat. Wasn't that fun? A little dangerous though.'

Edgar just stared at the red light, waiting for it to give way to green. There was no point encouraging his friend.

'No. It's not that kind of promise this time. I just want you to keep this code business between the two of us. Louise will kill me if she finds out I'm spending time on this instead of trying to land paying clients, but I just can't resist the challenge.'

'I know you can't, mate. Don't worry. I'll keep it quiet. Just crack the code as quickly as you can.'

Oscar looked at the clock on the sandstone tower of the city hall. It was ten past six. He turned his attention back to the sentence. He knew that if he hadn't worked it out by the end of the evening, he wouldn't be able to sleep all night.

'Edgar, how about you drive yourself home?'

'You don't want me to come back to your place?'

'I'm not going home just yet. I need some time alone to think. I might go for a quiet stroll around York's Hollow.'

'You and your York's Hollow! I sometimes reckon you think you have Turrbal blood flowing through your veins.'

'Well, I can understand why it was so important to them. The place exudes tranquillity.'

Oscar looked at the part of the sentence that had been underlined again: "The means which his Excellency placed at my disposal were well calculated to attain…"

Then he read the coded message, thinking carefully about the last line:

The Stayne family fortune is built on a foundation of betrayal and sin. We must come together to put right all the wrong that has been done. The family knows that I have proof of its evil deeds and is watching me. Page twenty-five holds the key. 5 and 9 is 1 and 2, the last 4 come last.

4.

'Where's Osky?' Helen asked Louise as she poured herself another glass of pinot noir. She knew Oscar hated being called that but figured it didn't matter when he wasn't around.

'I don't know. He's probably off on a case. It's been pretty quiet recently, but I don't dare suggest he get a "real" job.'

'He's a genius when it comes to solving unusual crimes. I'm sure he could do just about any job he set his mind to, but I can't imagine him being satisfied doing anything else.'

'You know what? Sometimes I wish he wasn't as smart as he is.'

'You don't mean that.'

'I do, really. It would be easier if he just got a normal job and lived a normal life.'

'Yeah'? And watched the footy on Friday night, and drank beer all day with his mates on Saturday, and drove a Monaro?'

'Maybe not *that* normal!'

'You wouldn't love him any other way than how he is right now.'

Louise smiled. 'I suppose you're right.'

'Hello?' a voice called from the direction of the open front door.

'Who's that?' Helen asked, almost whispering.

'I don't know.'

'Is anybody home?' It was the voice of an elderly lady.

'Yes, I'm coming!' Louise called out. She frowned at Helen and shrugged.

The woman at the door was small and seemed to be a little confused. She smiled apologetically at Louise.

'I'm sorry to disturb you, dear, but I'm looking for Mr Tremont.'

'Aren't we all?'

'Excuse me?'

'Never mind. He's not here at the moment. I'm his wife. Perhaps I can take a message for him.'

'Yes, of course.' She adjusted her thick glasses so she could see Louise more clearly. 'It's about a theft. Some of my jewellery has gone missing and I can't for the life of me understand how it's possible. I always keep the house locked up when I go out, and I'm at home most of the time anyway.'

'My husband will certainly be able to help you. What was your name?'

'Simmons. Vera Simmons.'

'If you give me your phone number, I'll have Oscar contact you in the morning. Just give me a moment to find a pen.'

Louise dashed into the kitchen and took a pen and sheet of note paper from on top of the fridge.

Mrs Simmons gave Louise her number and bid her a good evening. She then shuffled back off the verandah, descending the steps carefully.

Louise smiled to herself as she switched the outside light on to make her visitor's departure safer. A real client—just what they needed.

#

Oscar didn't get home until almost ten o'clock. Helen had gone home and his wife had fallen asleep in front of a French movie.

He'd watched the sun set behind the trees surrounding the pond in York's Hollow. Ducks and water fowl chased each other through the rushes and lilies that flourished in the shallow water, and a constant, gentle breeze rustled the leaves overhead. Of course, the Turrbal people no longer camped in the gully they called Barrambin. Nowadays, the only people passing by were cyclists speeding along the bike path separating the hollow from the Victoria Park golf course.

Oscar was glad to find that Louise was asleep on the sofa. That meant his explanations could wait until morning. So, after quietly brushing his teeth and slipping into his pyjamas, he climbed into bed. But he soon realised he wasn't going to be able to fall asleep at the drop of a hat.

He stared at the ceiling of his bedroom and saw the words of the sentence fragment write themselves in bright white letters. At the same time, he recalled the final instructions of the code. The answer was there in front of his eyes.

Oscar knew he was capable of cracking a simple riddle. All

he needed to do was decipher and follow the instructions.

The words rewrote themselves over and over again, but at some point in time they vanished. Sleep had claimed him.

5.

'Hello, Mrs Simmons. My wife told me you need help with a little mystery—Yes, I can come over now. Your address is?—Yes, I think so. Near the bridge across Kedron Brook?—I'll be there in about ten minutes.'

Vera Simmons' house was a typical post-war cottage with a living room at the front and a hallway leading past two bedrooms to the kitchen, dining room, and bathroom at the back. The entire house reeked of lavender oil, and horrible china dolls in lace dresses stood guard in random places, including on top of the television cabinet and on the telephone stand in the hallway.

'Would you like a cup of tea, Mr Tremont?'

'Yes, please. Do you have herbal tea?'

Mrs Simmons frowned, making her chunky glasses push forward a little on her nose. '*Herbal* tea?' she repeated to herself. 'I'm afraid not, just Earl Grey.'

'A cup of Earl Grey will do fine.' He didn't want to be impolite.

'Milk?'

He hesitated. 'Yes, please. A cloud of milk. No sugar.'

He followed her into the kitchen.

'You live alone, Mrs Simmons?'

'Yes, but I have two sons who live nearby. They come and see me almost every weekend.'

'Do you have anybody else who comes to your house regularly? Is there somebody who helps with the housework, for example?'

She handed him his cup of tea.

He took a sip. It wasn't so bad after all.

'No, I do all my housework myself. Nobody comes into the house much, and only when I'm here. I always lock up whenever I go out. That's why I came to you. I really don't understand how anybody could have stolen my jewellery.'

'Show me where you keep your valuables.'

She led him through to her bedroom. It was very neat, with lace curtains hanging in front of the sole window and paintings of rural homesteads on the walls. The only items of furniture—other than the bed—were an imitation Edwardian wardrobe and matching duchess.

Oscar walked over to the casement window and pushed both panes open.

'I can't imagine anybody climbing up this high,' she said.

'You'd be surprised what professional burglars are capable of, Mrs Simmons. That said, I do agree with you. These windows would be very difficult to open from the outside without causing any damage to the framework, and you are adamant that you keep them closed when you're not at home.'

Oscar didn't like the look of this case. He already had the feeling he was going to end up telling Mrs Simmons he wouldn't be able to get to the bottom of it. Burglaries with no clues were extremely difficult to solve, unless the stolen goods could be located. But that took a lot of patience and even more luck.

'This is where you keep your jewellery?' Oscar pointed to a small silver box sitting on her duchess, perfectly aligned with her hairbrush and three bottles of perfume. A few items of jewellery were sitting on the duchess around the box—one pair of opal earrings and a matching necklace.

She nodded.

'Only one pair of earrings is missing?'

'That's right,' she admitted, unaware of the real reason Oscar had asked that question.

'May I have a look inside?'

'Of course.'

Oscar opened the hinged lid of the jewellery box. There were several pieces that must have been worth a substantial sum of money, including a splendid diamond ring. He reached in and removed the ring. He lifted it up to the window so he could see it clearly.

'That ring was given to me by my mother-in-law on my twentieth wedding anniversary. Thank heavens the burglar didn't steal that one!'

Oscar turned his gaze thoughtfully from the ring to Mrs Simmons. Then he placed it back in the silver box.

'That's precisely what I find difficult to understand. Why didn't he take all of your valuable jewellery? It doesn't make sense to steal just one pair of earrings and leave everything else.'

'I suppose you're right. I didn't think about that.'

Oscar finished his cup of tea and stroked his moustache. He looked around the bedroom again.

'Mrs Simmons, I notice some of your jewellery is sitting on your duchess instead of being kept in the jewellery box. Why is that?'

She looked at the duchess and squinted through her glasses, then took a step forward so she could see the items he was talking about.

'Oh, you mean those? Well, I wore them yesterday. I was wearing them when I went to your house yesterday evening.'

'So, do you often keep jewellery you've just worn sitting on the duchess?'

She hesitated. 'Yes, I do. What difference does that make though? Will that help you find the burglar?'

Oscar smiled. 'I don't know about that, but it will definitely help me solve this mystery.' He was starting to regain his self-confidence. 'When did you last see the missing earrings?'

'It must have been Monday morning. I wore them to a meeting in the city. I wanted to dress up.'

'Monday morning,' Oscar repeated. 'Then, when you got home, did you put them on the duchess or in the jewellery box?'

She looked lost for a moment. 'I really can't remember. I didn't pay much attention to what I did with them.'

'It was yesterday that you realised they'd gone missing?'

'Yes. I think so. No, it was Tuesday. Or was it? I'm not sure, to tell the truth.'

'Don't worry. It probably isn't important.'

Oscar walked around the room, inspecting it in silence.

'Your bedroom is very clean. You said you do all your housework yourself?'

Mrs Simmons nodded.

'It's not difficult with your short-sightedness?'

'It can be sometimes, but I get by.'

He looked at the carpet. It appeared to be quite clean. He knelt down and examined it more closely. It was impeccable.

'When did you last vacuum the floor?'

'I generally do it every second day. I know it's a bit excessive, but I like to keep my house as clean as a whistle. Oh dear, I've probably erased some important clues, haven't I?'

'Clues?' Oscar asked, getting back to his feet. 'No, I don't think you've done any harm. However, I would quite like to see your vacuum cleaner if you don't mind.'

'Of course. Follow me.'

She led him through to the kitchen, where the vacuum cleaner was stowed away behind the door, next to the refrigerator.

'I do hope you'll find a clue inside. How about I make you another cup of tea?'

'That would be lovely, Mrs Simmons,' Oscar answered, and he removed the dust bag from the vacuum cleaner. 'I'll just take this outside so I don't get any dust on the floor.'

He disappeared down the staircase leading from the kitchen to the backyard, and by the time Mrs Simmons had begun pouring the tea, he was on his way back up.

'Did you find a clue then, Mr Tremont?'

He held his right hand out. It was clenched into a fist and the three long scars it had carried since childhood blazed like mischievous grins.

'A clue, indeed!' he announced triumphantly, taking Mrs Simmons by surprise and almost causing her to drop one of the teacups.

He unclenched his fist slowly, and she took a step towards him.

'My earrings! You've found them!'

'I most certainly have. It seems your humble vacuum cleaner has been stealing from you.'

He handed them to her.

'Thank you so much!'

'It's a pleasure.'

She stared at them absently for a moment.

'Oh, now I understand. They must have fallen off my duchess. Later, when I cleaned my room, I failed to notice them.'

'That's exactly what happened. There was no thief after all.

I was worried for a minute that Brisbane had suddenly become home to the world's greatest cat burglar.'

'How silly it was of me, Mr Tremont. Here I was dreaming up all kinds of far-fetched ideas when it was just a simple case of carelessness. I often do that, you know. I overcomplicate things when the solution is right there in front of me, and instead of thinking about it too much, I should just accept the simplest solution.'

Oscar nodded and sipped thoughtfully at his cup of tea. Then his expression changed.

'That's it!' he exclaimed.

'What's what?'

I should just accept the simplest solution. Those were her very words.

'Thank you. You're absolutely right. Why make matters more complicated than they really are? I'm sorry, Mrs Simmons, but I have to go.'

Oscar put the teacup on the kitchen bench and darted back through the house and out to his car.

Keep it simple. That was the key!

5 and 9 is 1 and 2, the last 4 come last.

6.

Oscar sat on his thinking chair and followed the line with his index finger.

"The means which his Excellency placed at my disposal were well calculated to attain…"

5 and 9 is 1 and 2—e, w. *The last 4 come last*—t, a, i, n.

'Ewtain?' he mouthed to himself. That made no sense.

Maybe 5 and 9 referred to the fifth and ninth words of the text—*Excellency* and *disposal*. If so, why specify that these words should be first and second, and that the last four must come last? Surely that was clear.

He repeated the instructions to himself in his mind.

Maybe they were letters, *first* and *second*. In *Excellency*, the first letter was *E*, and in *disposal*, the second was *i*, and the last four letters of the last four words came to *l*, *d*, *o*, *n*.

'Eildon!' He almost sprang from his thinking chair.

He felt a shiver of excitement course through his body. He'd finally cracked it. It had been so simple after all. He felt like kicking himself.

Eildon Hill was the answer. That was where whoever was intended to read the code was supposed to meet the sender. The only question was; how many years ago did all this happen, if at all?

Oscar strode through his house and over to the living room window. He looked out across Wilston towards the plateau that dominated the north of Brisbane. Beyond the rusty Hills Hoist and the pawpaw trees that stood in his backyard, and the corrugated roofs of his neighbours' homes, he could see Eildon Hill, covered in trees and crowned with a mobile phone tower. But he knew it had not always looked like that. Back in the days when the north of Brisbane was being settled, it had been a mostly bare hill surrounded by just a handful of large stately houses. Then, in the late twenties, it was turned into a water reservoir.

What was the connection with a wealthy family called the Staynes?

Oscar didn't know the answer, but he knew where he could find it. He grabbed his car keys.

#

The former Windsor Town Council Chambers building was built of stone cut from the old quarry that rose directly behind it. The small building was a reminder of the era when the suburb had been a town in its own right.

Oscar stepped through its arched doorway and into the small office that housed the Windsor Historical Society.

The little man wearing long sleeves and a green cardigan looked up and smiled at Oscar. His was the kind of warm, welcoming countenance the detective immediately recognised as the sign of someone who is bored to tears and hoping for a chat. It was just the reception Oscar had hoped for.

'Good morning,' he said.

'Good morning. My name is Oscar Tremont and I'm doing a spot of research on the history of the local area. I thought you might be able to help me.'

'Of course, I can help you. That's what the Windsor and Districts Historical Society is all about. My name is Peter Fossick. Did you say your name was Oscar Tremont?'

Oscar regretted his mistake instantly. He wanted to make enquiries without drawing attention to himself. He'd given the gentleman his name as an act of courtesy, but he hadn't expected him to recognise it. His reputation was obviously more widespread than he'd thought.

'Yes, that's right,' he confirmed.

'The investigator of strange happenings?'

Oscar forced a smile. 'That's me.'

'You're here on a case then?'

'No, I'm just here out of personal interest.' He wasn't lying, after all.

'Oh, I see.' The man was evidently disappointed. 'Well,

how can I help you?'

Oscar decided not to mention the Staynes outright. He didn't want to give his game away entirely. Ideally, he would find a way to manipulate Mr Fossick into volunteering the name of the family in question.

'I'm interested in the founding families of Windsor and Wilston. For example, could you tell me about the families behind the area's stately homes, like Boothville, Oakwal, and Kirkston?'

'With pleasure. Let's see. Well, how about we start with Boothville?'

Oscar nodded and listened intently for several minutes as the local historian rattled off the names of early bankers, solicitors, and judges who had built grand houses on the hills of the towns that later became the suburbs of Windsor and Wilston. There was no mention of the Stayne family. Oscar would have to attack from another angle.

'Were there other grand houses around the area?'

'Oh yes. There were several. Let me think.'

Oscar waited patiently.

'There was one close to Eildon Hill, on Constitution Road.'

'What was it called?'

'Stayne House. It was named after the family that built it.'

'That sounds interesting. Who were they, these Skains?'

'Staynes,' Mr Fossick said, correcting Oscar's fabricated mistake. 'They were one of Brisbane's wealthiest families at the turn of the century. They owned much of the city and all of Eildon Hill.'

'Were they influential?'

'Funny you should ask. Despite their immense wealth, they didn't participate much in community life. They were quite reserved. In those days, wealthy families were expected to play a major role in society and politics. The Staynes' reclusiveness did them no credit.'

'The house no longer exists?'

'No. I'm not sure what happened to it, but I could find out for you. Are you a member of the Historical Society?'

'I'm considering joining. I wonder if the family still lives in the area.'

'I don't know. The White Pages would be the best way to check that.'

'Quite right. What was the nature of the other property the family owned around Brisbane?'

'They had money invested in everything from Queen Street retail shops to shipping companies, and they helped finance the Queensland Museum and Exhibition Hall.'

'The Old Museum?'

'That's right, but they weren't involved in running it. It was a purely financial investment, from what I understand.'

'Thank you, Mr Fossick. That's very interesting. I'll be in touch soon.'

'If you become a member, you can gain access to our archives.'

'That's a good idea. I'll get back to you. Thanks again.'

Back in his car, Oscar reclined his seat so he could relax and think about what he'd learned.

Did the reference to *Eildon* mean the opponents of the Stayne family had launched a plot to enter the house in order to procure something the family had wanted to keep hidden? What could they have been after? What did the family have to hide? The coded message had accused them of acquiring their wealth through betrayal and sin. Was the powerful family's tendency to remain out of the social and political spotlight an admission of a collective guilty conscience?

Oscar had so many questions to answer, but the challenge didn't daunt him. He was determined to get to the bottom of it all. The first questions he needed to answer were: Did the Stayne family still live in the area? And, if so, what did they know about their history?

7.

Jasmine lashed out again. It was often on evenings like this—once the sun had set and the moon was full—that the devil came.

'Tighten the straps!'

Rebecca jerked the end of the thick leather strap loose and then pulled with all the strength she could muster, but her sister's body was more powerful and the strap started to slacken.

'Pull, Becky!' her father ordered.

'I can't. She's too strong. She's getting stronger each time.'

Rebecca was right. Jasmine was already considerably more powerful than most fourteen-year-old girls. The changes that were happening to her weren't due to puberty and raging hormones—there were far more sinister forces at work.

Eamon Wight finished tightening the strap on his side of the bed, his strong fingers working quickly, like the legs of a spider binding a newly caught fly to its web. Then he leaped around the bed to Rebecca's side just in time to stop the strap from being pulled completely loose by Jasmine, who was thrashing with all her might and spitting foul curses.

'Fuck you!' the deep voice growled. It was a curse from the putrid depths of a bottomless pit, not the rebellious swearing of an adolescent girl.

'Be quiet, Satan!' Eamon commanded, and he buckled the

strap.

His daughter was now secure.

'Come on, daddy! Do me! I know you want to! You have ever since mummy pissed off and left you all alone. You think about it all the time, don't you?'

'Go back to hell, Satan!'

Eamon reached into the front right pocket of his trousers and removed a silver crucifix. It glinted in the dim light provided by a lamp that stood on a low table at a safe distance from the bed.

Jasmine's pale face twisted into a grotesque grimace and her back arched so high she looked like a bridge. Only her hands, feet, and head remained on the bed.

Her father approached her.

'You'll do it one day, daddy. You know that. Even *you* can't resist temptation for ever.'

She spat at the crucifix as it came rushing down towards her, but she missed. It kissed her forehead and she thrashed even harder than before, trying to get away. Then she closed her wild brown eyes, feigning submission.

'Rebecca, close the window for Christ's sake! We don't want the neighbours to hear us.'

'Blasphemer! You're a blasphemer, daddy!'

Rebecca was shaking, even though she'd already taken part in the exorcism of her younger sister several times over the last few months. She would never get used to it, and she was afraid Jasmine would never really be her sister again.

'Don't close the window! What are you trying to hide? Domestic violence, you shit? Ashamed of how you treat your daughter, are you?'

Rebecca pulled the window closed and locked the interior wooden shutters.

'You whore, Rebecca! Open the window! I need fresh air.'

'There's plenty of air in here.'

'Don't talk to her!' Eamon ordered, turning to Rebecca. 'Not when she's like this.'

'You pathetic man! You couldn't even keep your own wife! You must have a tiny dick!'

'Rebecca, go downstairs, please.'

'No, Rebecca, don't leave me with him. He does all kinds of horrible things to me when you're away.'

Rebecca hesitated for a moment.

'Rebecca, go downstairs,' her father pleaded. 'I don't want you listening to the devil's filth. It will corrupt your soul.'

'Hypocrite! She's not *that* stupid. She knows why you want her to go downstairs.'

Rebecca shuddered as she took one last glance at the thing that was usually her sister before rushing out of the room.

Eamon concentrated on the exorcism again. He wasn't a priest; his brother, Sean, had been the one to pursue that career, until some unfortunate events had forced him to make a timely departure in order to appease public and hierarchical pressure. Eamon had chosen a more practical line of work, becoming a plumber. He'd learned about exorcisms from his brother, one of a handful of people who knew the family's terrible secret. Performing an exorcism wasn't all that different from plumbing really; they were both just a matter of cleaning the shit out of a system.

He applied the crucifix to her forehead, and she hissed in reply and then farted loudly. Undeterred, he repeated some lines from the Bible that he'd been told were especially despicable for demons to hear. He knew them by heart now. He even whispered them to himself when he was at work, unclogging the pipes under kitchen sinks or thrusting a plunger into a blocked toilet. Once, Miss Yates, whose pipes had seemed to need cleaning unusually frequently, had heard him repeating lines from the Good Book to himself while his head was hidden under a sink. Her warm, flirty attitude towards him had quickly changed after that. Since then, her pipes hadn't needed much attention.

'You're a loser, Eamon!'

He hated it when his daughter called him by his first name. He had to remind himself that it wasn't her who was speaking.

'Be quiet, Satan! God commands you to still your serpent tongue!'

'You failed as a husband, and now you're failing as a father!'

Eamon kept the crucifix held against her forehead and repeated the verses more loudly. Little by little, Jasmine's body relaxed and her gaze changed.

'Daddy?' The voice was sweet again. 'Untie me, please! My wrists hurt so much.'

The innocent face looking at him pouted. He never could resist it when his daughters stuck their bottom lips out. 'He's gone now, daddy. It's me again.'

Eamon looked at his daughter. She'd stopped struggling. She lay there, strapped to the bed like a defenceless animal in a poacher's trap. His heart filled with pity. The devil had finally gone. Jasmine's episodes were getting longer and more violent each time. He wondered how long he would be able to perform the exorcisms himself. His brother told him he needed a real exorcist, but Eamon didn't want the Church to know about this family shame. His brother had already caused enough embarrassment.

'Daddy?' she said, cocking her head to one side.

He took a step closer, fighting back tears. He sometimes

wondered whether the horrible words Jasmine's mouth spoke when she was possessed came straight from the devil inside her or from deep within her mind. He hoped that it was only the former. He wouldn't have been able to survive if he'd believed for an instant that his daughter could have thought such things about him.

'Daddy's here, honey. You're better now. It's all over.'

8.

'You're working on a case, aren't you?'

Oscar looked up from his laptop and took a sip of whisky so he had an excuse for not answering his wife's question immediately.

'You are. I know it.' She smiled.

He tilted his head to one side—a gesture she knew meant, *I can't pull the wool over your eyes, sweetheart.*

'That's great! What is it?'

He couldn't tell her it was just a matter of curiosity, but he didn't want to lie to her either.

'It's a long story and I really need to make some progress on it tonight. Can I tell you about it tomorrow?'

Louise shrugged. '*Très bien, mon amour.* I'll let you continue. I'm going to bed. *Bonne nuit.*'

Oscar certainly did need to make some progress if he was going to justify persisting with the cold case. The further he ventured, the more it seemed he was heading for a dead end. He'd searched for the Stayne family of Brisbane on every website imaginable but was constantly overwhelmed by the absence of results.

He sipped his whisky and sat back, wondering how he could hope to discover the dark secret of a family that had seemingly disappeared from the city decades ago. Had they all gone somewhere else, or had they somehow managed to make themselves completely inaccessible without leaving Brisbane? In either case, was it reasonable to presume that a sense of guilt lay behind the decision? The questions kept coming, filing through Oscar's mind like soldiers on parade.

He didn't like working on assumptions, but they were all he had. The facts were too scarce. One fact he was sure of was that the family's original home had been demolished long ago and any proof of wrongdoing it had contained had either been destroyed with it or taken elsewhere. But he had no leads to follow at all. Whoever had written the coded message had claimed to possess proof of the family's sins, but Oscar didn't know the identity of this person or even when the code had been written. For the first time in his career, he felt completely lost. He thanked goodness he didn't have a client he was letting down, just himself and his damned curiosity.

Eildon. That was the key to the mystery. Stayne House had once stood upon Eildon Hill—a majestic colonial homestead towering over the modern day suburbs of Windsor, Wilston, and The Grange. The family had then acquired even greater wealth, enough to enable the Staynes to invest in some of Brisbane's most promising commercial and cultural projects, such as the Old Museum. If their wealth had been obtained through dishonest means, as "betrayal and sin" clearly suggested, surely it was probable that their victim—or victims—had been other wealthy families living nearby.

Oscar sat up straight and opened a new page on his web browser. He placed his fingers on the keyboard and stared at them for a few long seconds, then he typed a string of words with lightning speed; *fall doom curse family Eildon Hill.*

The results were as strange as the words he'd chosen, but as he sorted through them, he noticed one name frequently popping up.

9.

Noreen O'Connell opened the door with a bewildered look on her face. She wasn't used to having visitors so early in the morning. She hadn't even finished her breakfast.

The chubby man at the door pushed the glasses slipping down his sweaty nose back up and smiled. He wore an atrocious checked jacket and corduroy trousers that were at least two sizes too small for him.

'Good morning?'

'Good morning, Mrs—' He referred to his clipboard. 'Mrs O'Connell?'

'That's right, and you are?'

'Mr Newbury of the Queensland Genealogical Society. I trust I'm not disturbing you.'

She felt like telling him he was and that she hadn't finished her marmalade on toast yet, but he seemed like such a nice man, and he wasn't trying to sell anything—or was he?

'Are you trying to sell something?' she asked.

He chuckled heartily, as though it was the funniest thing he'd heard in a long time. The chuckle slipped into a kind of snort, and then he gave her a wink.

She smiled. Despite his chubbiness and horrible dress sense, he was quite a charming young man—*young* being under sixty by Mrs O'Connell's interpretation of the word.

'Not at all,' he confirmed. 'I don't want a red cent, just a little information. The society is currently conducting a study of the area's history.'

'Well, I can't help you there. As you can no doubt tell by

my accent, I'm from Ireland originally. I moved into this house eight years ago. My husband and I don't know a great deal about local history, I'm afraid.'

'Yes, of course.' He nodded, and his glasses slipped down his nose again. 'Do you know your neighbours very well?'

Mrs O'Connell looked towards the houses that flanked her own. She was obviously going through the inhabitants of each one, estimating how long they'd lived in the neighbourhood.

'We're particularly interested in the descendants of the Staynes.'

She shook her head.

Oscar pushed the glasses back up his nose. The disguise may not have been necessary, but he preferred to play it safe. He had a reputation in that part of town, as Mr Fossick had reminded him. Going incognito was always a good idea when there was even a slight possibility that revealing your identity could lead to trouble.

'What about the Wight family?'

'Wight, you say? That name rings a bell.'

Oscar let her think for a moment.

'Look, I'm really not sure. I think there's a Wight family around here, but I can't say for certain. You should try Helen, at number 109. She knows everybody in the street.'

'I'll do that. Thank you very much for your help.'

The chubby man nodded politely and made his way along the garden path and back onto the street. Parents were dropping their children off at the local school. He knew it wasn't the best time to knock on people's doors, but he couldn't wait until evening. The urge to make progress wouldn't let him waste a single minute of his day.

He pushed the gate to 109 open and walked up to the front door. It was open and he could hear voices coming from inside. He listened for a moment, trying to hear what was being said. Experience had taught him the best answers were given when no questions have been asked. But he couldn't hear well enough to understand.

Suddenly, the sound of footsteps on polished wood rang out. He pressed the doorbell so it wouldn't seem that he was snooping around.

'Mum, there's someone at the door!' a blue-clad child called out.

'I know, Ben. Get your lunch from the fridge.'

A tall, elegant woman appeared at the door. She was obviously getting ready for work, and Oscar could sense she wouldn't have the time or inclination to chat.

'Yes? Can I help you?'

'Good morning, I'm from the Queensland Genealogical Society and I just wanted to ask you a couple of quick questions about your family's history.'

'I'm sorry, but I'm in a hurry. Can you come back some other time?'

Oscar wasn't giving up so easily. 'Could you give me your name? Maybe I can tell you something about your family history.'

'No, I will not give you my name, and anyway, my family has no history in this part of the country.'

She turned to walk back inside.

'Could you tell me if you know anything about the Stayne family?'

She spun around and frowned at him. 'There is no Stayne family in this area.'

'There used to be,' Oscar told her.

'No, there has never been anyone by that name in this street,' she contradicted him.

Oscar was speechless. It seemed she'd taken his suggestion as a personal insult.

'What about the Wight family?' He'd decided to push her buttons.

She glared at him.

'The Wights?' She paused. 'No, I don't know any Wights. Now, please leave!'

Oscar thanked her humbly and turned around.

As he walked back towards the garden gate, he noticed that he couldn't hear her high-heels tapping against the polished wood floor. That could only mean one thing. Helen wasn't hurrying back inside. She was watching him leave.

He'd got her worried.

A playful smile crept onto his face.

#

Rebecca Wight had grabbed her schoolbag and was just leaving the house when her path was blocked by a strange man carrying a clipboard. Oscar realised instantly that his arrival had caused the teenage girl to panic, and panic meant the inability to think clearly. He had her at a disadvantage. Although he had no idea whose house he was at, he figured it was worth taking a stab in the dark.

'Hello, Miss Wight. I'm from the Queensland Genealogical Society. Would your mum or dad be home by any chance?'

'No,' she replied warily. 'Dad's gone to work already.'

Bingo!

'Never mind. I'll come back later. Do you know what time he'll be back?'

'He probably won't be here until around four thirty or five. You would just be wasting your time though. He doesn't like to have visitors.'

Oscar smiled charmingly in order to catch the girl off guard with his next question. 'Mr Wight has something to hide, does he?'

Her panic deepened, but she forced herself to say, 'No, he has nothing to hide. That's not a nice thing to say.'

Oscar smiled sympathetically. 'Of course not, dear. That's just my poor sense of humour. I had better let you hurry along to school. Thanks for your time.'

He turned, walked back to the street, and pretended to be on his way.

10.

Conventional wisdom has it that it takes a thief to catch a thief, and while Oscar Tremont was an investigator who always strove to do what he believed to be right, he was by no means a stranger to the arts of the master burglar. If he was going to get to the bottom of this mystery, he would have to take some risks, and if the Wight family was the victim of bygone injustice, he had a moral obligation to set the record straight. To help them, he would have to enter their home illegally. There were no ifs or buts about it. He would have to do his utmost to discover whether there was anything in their house that could confirm the notion that the Stayne family had done them wrong.

Oscar watched Rebecca stroll away from the other side of the street. She didn't look back.

Once she was far enough away, he returned to the gate of the house and pretended to read his clipboard so that any observers would assume he was at the address on official business. He then walked quickly but calmly around to the back. There was a tangle of shrubs and vines growing in the garden, and neither the Wights nor any of the neighbouring households seemed to have dogs. It was perfect. Oscar looked around casually to check that he wasn't being watched.

He reached into his jacket pocket and removed a fine metallic instrument which he proceeded to slide into the keyhole of the back door. He toyed with the pick for a few seconds and then heard the lock click. It was a piece of cake. He donned a pair of thin rubber gloves and pushed the door open. He crept through the laundry, past the washing machine and a shelf full of cleaning domestic products and gardening tools. An open door led him into the kitchen, which was absolutely spotless. Miss Wight had either done her washing-up after breakfast or hadn't had any breakfast at all. But it wasn't the kitchen that interested him. He knew his best bet would be the study. If there wasn't one, then the living room or a bedroom would be the next most likely places to discover personal information.

He moved through the house so quietly the ticking of the living room clock was the loudest sound to be heard. He scanned everywhere, searching simultaneously for signs of an alarm system, any indication that somebody might still be at home, and a cabinet or chest of drawers that seemed like the kind of place important family documents would be kept.

There was a wooden chest sitting inconspicuously between the sofa and the bay window. It was just the kind of vessel people had the habit of using to keep their personal souvenirs—safe but within arm's reach. He walked over to it and knelt, and although he tried to keep his senses alert, for a moment, the only three things that existed in his world were his gloved hands, the wooden chest, and the ticking clock. The chest wasn't locked. He lifted the lid carefully and removed the ridiculous glasses from his face so he could examine the contents properly. It was full of old fishing and camping magazines.

He lowered the lid and stood. The next step was to locate another potential depository of family history. He couldn't give up after just one attempt. Then, just as he was glancing through the window to check that there was nobody raising the alarm outside, something happened that gave him the biggest fright he'd had since the night he was sleeping in a supposedly haunted house and a possum fight suddenly erupted in the attic. Only, this was no possum. It was the voice of an adolescent girl.

'Who's down there? Is that you, Becky?'

He was sure he'd hardly made a sound.

'You should be at school.'

He walked back through the living room and towards the door to the garden, but the voice called out again.

'It's not *you*, is it? Are you a thief?'

He felt the urge to respond, letting her know he wasn't a thief.

'Come upstairs. Come and talk to me. Don't ignore me. I know you're there.'

Oscar's curiosity took control. She didn't sound distressed by the presence of a thief—why? She even wanted to engage him in conversation—why? She wasn't at school—why?

'Why won't you answer me?'

'I'm coming up,' he replied.

He turned on his heels and walked casually over to the internal staircase. It led up to an unusual darkness that defied the clear morning sky outside, and he had the impression all the upstairs doors and windows were closed. His nerves warned him of danger as he crept up the stairs, but his mind insisted that he was safe. After all, he was just going to have a chat with a teenage girl.

At the top of the staircase was a short corridor. It was about four metres long and led to a bathroom at the end. On either side was a door. On the door to the right, there was a small sign with a pink floral design framing the name, Rebecca. On the door to the left, there was a piece of cardboard. It read, Spare Room. Oscar reached out for the spare room's doorknob.

'I'm opening the door.'

'Yes, come in,' she replied. The girl's voice was soft and timid, yet strangely relaxed. It sounded as though, as far as she was concerned, there was nothing disturbing about inviting a burglar into the privacy of her bedroom.

He turned the doorknob with one hand and clasped one end of his clipboard with the other. It wasn't exactly a formidable weapon, but if he was walking into a trap, he could use it to defend himself. The end of a clipboard crashing into someone's throat at high speed would cause enough pain to give him time to escape.

But there was no trap. Oscar found himself in a dim bedroom with no natural light, just a small reading lamp. A teenage girl was sitting on a bed with her legs crossed and her back against the wall. The scene filled him with pity, not apprehension. She looked at him vacantly, as though the wind had blown a fly in through the window, and for a horrible instant, he felt like a ghost. He didn't exist. Then Oscar realised that if he'd been a fly, entering her cold sanctuary by the window, she probably would have been very surprised indeed, because the bedroom window was nowhere to be seen, hidden behind an internal shutter that was fastened with a padlock. Had the shutter been placed there to protect her from the outside world? It didn't seem to make sense. The door downstairs hadn't been secured in any serious way. Any burglar worth his salt could have picked the lock, even if he couldn't have done it as quickly as Oscar.

He turned around, glancing at the girl on the bed as he did so, and looked at the door. He went to close it, moving slowly.

That's when she said precisely what he'd expected.

'I wouldn't do that if I were you. The door locks when you close it. It can only be opened from the outside.'

He frowned, pretending not to understand, but the situation couldn't have been clearer. The teenage girl was locked up like the Prisoner of Chillon. She was trapped in her room all day while her sister went to school and carried out a normal life. There was very little furniture in her room, and there were huge dents in the walls, as well as long fingernail scratch marks that ruined the paintwork. A painting of the Virgin Mary was fixed to the wall with more than a dozen nails, as was a large crucifix at the head of her bed. The bed itself looked more like a mediaeval instrument of torture than the soft nest of an adolescent girl. Oscar could see that there were straps and cuffs attached to it. In one corner of the room was a box-shaped chair with a trapdoor in the middle of the seat and a roll of toilet paper sitting on the floor next to it. In the opposite corner was a small table with its legs bolted to the floor and a selection of basic food and drink on it.

The girl observed him as he glanced around the room. She was an attractive teenager, verging on womanhood, with small perky breasts pressing against her light nightgown. Her eyes were sad yet playful, and she was obviously happy to have some company, even if it was that of a podgy middle-aged representative of the Queensland Genealogical Society. She looked upwards, as though silently telling Oscar there was one direction he'd neglected in his perusal of her bedroom. He followed her gaze and saw what she was showing him.

A huge scarlet cross was painted across the ceiling, forming a permanent reminder. Whenever she woke up or lay down to sleep, she would see it there and remember that God was watching her.

Oscar had been confronted with an assortment of strange and disturbing situations as an investigator of the inexplicable, but he'd never come face to face with a sufferer of demonic possession.

'I'll keep the door open then.'

She nodded. 'You'd better, if you want to be able to leave again.'

'What about you? Don't you want to leave?'

'Of course not. Where would I go?'

The blank look on her face made Oscar feel uneasy.

'You could go to school with your sister, for a start.'

'You know Becky?'

'Yes, I do. Well, I met her outside as she was leaving to go to school.'

'I can't go to school, and you know very well why not. You know I'm cursed.'

'Cursed? That's not the word I would use. You have a sickness, and you need help. Your father isn't helping you by keeping you locked up in here.'

'My father is the only person I have. My mother walked out on us because of me. He does his best to look after Becky and me. It must be hard for a man to deal with two teenage girls all by himself, especially when one of them is, well, like me.'

Oscar clasped his hands over his mouth and breathed out. He could have done with a double whisky to help him deal with the situation.

'Can I sit next to you?' he asked.

She nodded and patted the bed. He shuffled across and sat with his back against the scratched wall, imitating the way she was sitting even to the point of crossing his legs like her.

'What's your name, Miss Wight?'

'Jasmine.'

'Jasmine. That's a lovely name.'

She smiled, and he could read her mind—*but I'm not a lovely girl.*

'Jasmine, don't you want to know my name? Don't you want to know what I'm doing in your house?'

She placed a hand on his knee and smiled at him. Oscar cringed, her touch making him feel uncomfortable. All the same, he didn't push her hand away.

'I don't need to know your name, or why you came here. The important thing is that you're here now. I like company.'

'That's exactly why you need to go to school, so you can socialise with people your own age.'

'I can't do that though, can I? What if he comes while I'm at school?'

'I don't understand,' he lied.

'The Devil,' she whispered, and squeezed his leg to emphasise the unholy name.

'You need expert help, Jasmine.'

'No. Daddy won't hear of it. If you insist on trying to get me to leave my room, I will have to ask you to leave.'

Oscar looked into her eyes. She wasn't joking. He was beginning to get on her nerves.

'Has anybody else in your family had problems with the Devil?'

'Yes,' Jasmine admitted. 'It's genetic.'

'Indeed.' Oscar didn't know much about possession, but he was quite sure it wasn't purported to be genetic. 'Did your mother suffer from the same condition?'

'No, it's not on my mother's side. It's on my father's. The last case before me was a few generations back.'

Oscar said nothing. He didn't want to seem too eager, even though he was confident Jasmine would tell him whatever he needed to know.

'Can you tell me about it? It sounds interesting.'

She frowned at him and removed her hand from his leg. He felt both relieved and disappointed.

'It's not so much interesting as horrible.'

'I'm sorry. That was a poor choice of words.'

Her frown disappeared. She put her hand back on his leg, this time further up his thigh.

'It was back in the early days, when Brisbane was still growing as a city. The Wight family was very influential. Can you imagine it?' Jasmine laughed. 'I've seen photos of her—my great-great grandmother, or was it my great-great-great grandmother? Anyway, she was an elegant woman—in the photos at least. She emigrated from Scotland with her husband and they settled in the area. Her husband was the first minister of the Windsor Presbyterian Church and owned most of Eildon Hill.'

'What happened?'

'We don't really know. I'm just telling you what my dad told us. He says the minister wanted to keep his wife's condition a secret from his congregation and the general public—for obvious reasons—and that he managed to do so for a while. A few years after their arrival in Brisbane, just as their family property was expanding and their sons were beginning careers, another local family discovered the secret.'

The pieces were all falling into place.

'This other family blackmailed your ancestors?'

Jasmine nodded and a veil of simmering anger descended over her face. For a terrifying instant, Oscar thought the girl was about to have a fit of some kind. He expected her voice to morph to that of a demon, and the hand that rested so gently on his lap to lash out, grabbing him by the testicles, holding him prisoner. He expected her to vomit all over him.

None of this happened. She was just a melancholy teenage girl telling him about her family history. But it wasn't just history to her—it was an ever-present part of her life, and she personally felt the wrong done to her forebears. Oscar looked at the cross painted on the ceiling. It was only natural that she felt as though history and the present were one and the same for her. She bore the legacy of her ancestors. Perhaps demonic possession was genetic after all.

Oscar shook his head. He didn't believe in demons, not supernatural ones at any rate. No. This poor girl had a psychological disorder of some kind, and she needed proper treatment. Locking people up in rooms may have been the usual way to deal with such matters in the nineteenth century, but it certainly wasn't nowadays.

'Yes. They blackmailed us.'

'And are they still blackmailing you today?'

Jasmine frowned. Either she was a superb actress or she was frankly surprised by Oscar's suggestion.

'No. Daddy just keeps me here for my own good. He's not trying to hide me because I embarrass him. He does it to protect me from the world.'

That's what he's brought you up to believe, Oscar thought. *He may even believe it himself. But it's not right.*

'Blackmail is a despicable crime,' he said, shaking his head. He wanted to keep her talking. 'Do you know about this blackmailing? What is the name of the family that blackmailed your ancestors?'

'The Staynes. Have you heard of them? They became one of Brisbane's most powerful families.'

'I have heard of them. They owned a lot of property on Queen Street and at the docks. They also largely funded the construction of the Old Museum.'

She nodded, rubbing his thigh as though rewarding an obedient dog.

He cringed.

'Do they still live in the area? I wonder if the descendants of the blackmailers know about the shameful story behind their family's wealth.'

She shook her head. 'The Stayne family has long since disappeared. We think they may have moved overseas.'

Oscar didn't agree with her. He had a feeling the Stayne family was closer than Jasmine and her family thought.

'So, it was with the money they obtained through blackmail that they were able to become powerful.'

'I think they were already rich. Our two families were the wealthiest in the Windsor area. However, once they discovered that the minister's wife suffered episodes of possession, there was a gradual but steady change until the Stayne family was the most influential in all of Brisbane and our property and influence was diminished until we had just one small cottage behind the Presbyterian Church.'

'That's disgraceful,' Oscar said.

'Daddy told me that a lot of family heirlooms, including very valuable jewellery, were handed over as part of the blackmailing. To this day, we don't know where these heirlooms are.'

Oscar thought about the message he'd found in the book at *Archives*. Somebody had known about the blackmailing and claimed to have proof. According to this person, the key to the mystery was *Eildon*. What did that really mean?

'Jasmine, did your family have a house on Eildon Hill?'

'They had one close to the hill, further up Constitution Road. It was near the old aboriginal burial grounds.'

'There are aboriginal burial grounds near Eildon Hill?'

She nodded. 'It was a sacred site to them. The house is no longer there. It was demolished years ago.'

'And I suppose the Stayne family had a house nearby.'

'Theirs was also demolished many years ago, before daddy was even born.'

'And nobody knows where the Stayne family went when they left the area?'

'They just vanished.'

Oscar paused and tapped his fingers against the clipboard.

'Let me ask you about your neighbours,' he said eventually.

She shrugged. 'I almost never leave the house. I know about my family's history, but I don't know anything about the neighbours.'

'You must know the names of some of them. Becky must go to school with some young people who live in Constitution Road.'

'Sure, but none of them are called Stayne.'

'No, I didn't expect they would be. What names do you know?'

'There's Daniel Matheson, who lives a few doors up. He's a friend of Becky's boyfriend, but daddy doesn't know she has one. His parents moved into the neighbourhood when we were in primary school. Then there's the Petersen family. I'm not sure where they live, but dad has done work on their house.'

Jasmine thought for a moment, then shook her head.

'Oh, and there's Tom and Kelly. They go to school with

Becky too, but we don't really know them very well. I don't know their family name.'

Oscar nodded. 'Thanks, Jasmine. What about further up the street, close to Eildon Hill? Do you know the families up there?'

She shook her head.

'You don't know Noreen or Helen?'

'I don't think so.'

Oscar slipped from the bed and wandered around. He was lost in thought for a while, but when he turned back to Jasmine, he clapped his hands as though he'd come to a final decision.

'Jasmine, I've thoroughly enjoyed talking to you and promise we'll meet again. However, I'm afraid I have to leave now. I have some work to do.'

'Don't leave me, please.'

'I have to go. I can't stay here with you all day. I have to get back to work.'

'Stay with me. I'll do whatever you want.'

'I can't, Jasmine. I'm sorry. Should I leave the door open?'

'No!' she shouted. Then she calmed down. 'Stop tempting me, please. Just go, but do come back soon.'

Oscar put his hand over his heart. 'You have my word, Jasmine. I'll come back to help you. I hope you'll recognise me.'

'You mean *remember*, not *recognise*,' she corrected him. 'And I will.'

'Quite right,' he said with a wink. 'I'll be back to help you one day very soon. That's a promise.'

He left the bedroom, glancing back at her one last time as he pulled the door shut and heard the lock slip into place.

11.

Oscar felt empty as he left the Wight home and returned to normality. Children were now at school, and mums and dads were all at work—doing regular jobs—while Jasmine sat locked up like a criminal. But he was intent on keeping his promise, and as quickly as possible.

While he walked, he wondered what he ought to do next. He figured breaking into Helen's house was out of the question. Walking past it couldn't do any harm though. He would look at the house and wait for it to inspire him. Its very presence would help him decide what course of action to pursue.

As he drew closer, he realised he wasn't the only one interested. A car was parked a little further up the street, under the shade of a leafy Moreton Bay fig tree, and somebody was sitting in it. The possibility that it was just a coincidence occurred to Oscar, but he hoped it wasn't. Had his visit bothered Helen even more than he thought it had? Could she have suspected he might come back? If so, what did she have to hide? Who was this man, sitting in his car, doing a bad job of acting as though he was minding his own business?

He had to let the man spot him. He had to make sure he knew he was interested in the house, but without letting him know he'd been seen.

Oscar smiled. This was what he loved most about his line of work—a good old-fashioned game of cat and mouse. It was going to be a blast.

Mr Newbury held his clipboard up in front of him as he approached the gate. He looked down at it, as though checking some details, and then pretended to be inspecting the house, without actually entering the property. He wanted to know whether the man in the car was taking the bait, but it would have been risky to look in his direction.

He needed a ploy. He knew plenty of those. It was just a matter of choosing the most appropriate one for the situation. He could have gone for something elaborate, like taking his mobile phone out and holding it up, pretending to be trying to get a signal. That would have given him a moment to surreptitiously look at the car. The only problem was that since he was right near the transmitters on Eildon Hill that ploy could raise suspicion in a clever observer. A simpler approach was in order.

He tilted his head back and then brought it lashing forwards, swinging to his left. The fake sneeze allowed him to catch a glimpse of the man in the car.

And catch him he did. He was in the process of taking photographs of Oscar with a professional camera sporting a monstrous zoom. Apparently, Helen had hired a second-rate private eye to keep a tab on her house and the strange little man from the Genealogical Society. Oscar felt like laughing, but didn't allow himself the luxury. If only the PI had known his target was none other than Oscar Tremont. If he had, he would surely have gone back to Helen and told her he had to decline the contract. There wasn't a PI in Brisbane who would have dared try to follow Oscar.

So, you're looking to play, are you?

Oscar turned to a blank sheet of paper on his clipboard and began writing. His message was short but sharp. It would only take a couple of seconds for his tail to read it, and it would guarantee that he followed Oscar. The note read, 'Helen, as per our conversation, I know that you have information on the Stayne family. I am onto them, and you.'

He ripped the page off, folded it twice, and put it in the

letterbox.

I'm ready. Are you? Without turning his attention to the car, Oscar walked away from the house and crossed the street. He didn't look. He didn't need to. He knew what was happening. The PI had put his camera away and placed his hand on the door handle, getting ready to dash over to the letterbox. He was watching Oscar cross the street, waiting patiently. Then, just as Oscar reached the corner with Jessop Street and started to walk down that steep slope, he jumped out of the car and hurried over to the letterbox. Now, he was reading the note. He was congratulating himself. He was getting back into his car and starting it up. Oscar was almost halfway down Jessop Street. The man was driving slowly, trying not to be too obvious. He was smart enough to keep his distance.

Oscar knew he had to catch this man and make him talk, and that meant getting him out of his car.

He turned right and looked back. A few moments later, the front of the car peeped around the corner. Oscar turned back and continued walking quickly but casually. It was perfect. The man was doing just what he wanted. There was nothing like the thrill of a good hunt, even when he was playing the part of the quarry. Oscar walked briskly along the leafy length of Tenth Avenue, past cottages with corrugated red roofs and picket fences. Then he turned left and crossed the street. He checked the time on his pocket watch. The next train was due in ten minutes. The man would be forced to leave his car at the station car park and continue tailing on foot. They would be as equals then, and the hunter would become the hunted.

Oscar crossed the footbridge to the platform and waited for the Beenleigh train. His tail parked in the car park but stayed in his car. That was normal. He would wait until the train was pulling into the station to get out and rush across the pedestrian bridge. Oscar knew how a decent PI acted, and this man, despite having parked too close to number 109 Constitution Road, hadn't made many rookie mistakes. He probably had some experience in the game. In fact, Oscar wondered whether he knew him. He needed to get a closer look. Once they were both on the train, that would be possible. Later, once they were both off the train, Oscar would lead the man into an isolated park and they would get very close indeed.

His tail still hadn't moved when the train came roaring around the bend in the line.

Hurry the hell up or you'll miss it!

There was still no movement from the car. Then the train blocked his view of the car park. Oscar ducked around behind the station ticket office and watched the staircase leading down to the platform. Still, no movement. Something had gone wrong. The game was over before it had even begun.

The car headed off, leaving Oscar alone and confused on the platform.

12.

Oscar was still walking home when the phone rang. It was Edgar. He wouldn't have called when he knew Oscar was busy with the case unless it was important.

'Hello, Ed. How's it going?'

'Not bad, mate. I've been doing a little research into the Stayne family and I think I might have something for you.'

Oscar could tell by the smugness in his friend's voice that he thought it was something big. He hoped he was right. Every time he thought he was about to have a breakthrough, something had gone wrong.

'Don't tell me you've unearthed the Stayne family?'

'I may have done just that.'

'Are you serious, Ed?'

'I'm not sure, but I noticed that one of the families living in Constitution Road looks a lot like the Staynes in hiding.'

'Don't tell me, they live at number 109?'

'Not quite. Number 109? Oh, that's where Todd and Helen Benison live. Todd went to school with Nathan.'

'How do you get this kind of information?'

'That's for me to know and you to find out, my friend.'

'*Touché!*' Oscar laughed, recognising one of his favourite taunts being thrown back at him. 'So, who is Nathan?'

'It's Nathan Taysen, to be precise. He and his family live in Constitution Road. You didn't meet them this morning?'

'Not everybody answered their doors, and I'm pretty sure that name isn't in the White Pages. Did you say Taysen?'

'That's right, genius. Have you heard that name before?'

'No, but it sounds familiar, doesn't it?

'What are you saying?' He could hear Edgar's grin in his voice.

'You have to admit it sounds a lot like Stayne after a bit of letter shifting.'

'Exactly! At least, that's what I thought. We can't both be wrong, can we?'

'That would take a hell of a celestial misalignment. Do you have anything else on the Taysen clan?'

'Just that they own a lot of property around town, like a chocolate shop on Queen Street and shares in the Old Museum. Does that sound familiar?'

Oscar smiled. 'What would I do without you, Ed?'

'You'd get there eventually, after a lot of messing around and doing things the old-fashioned way.'

'You can say that again. I've had an eventful day, but it

wasn't as productive as it should have been.'

'Eventful, you say?'

'Come over this evening and I'll tell you everything over a whisky. In the meantime, I'm going to follow your lead. I've already been in brief contact with the Benisons, and they definitely know that the Staynes—or Taysens—have a skeleton or two in the family closet. Thanks, Ed. You're a champ!'

Oscar hung up. He passed Zone Fresh, the small and rather expensive grocery shop where he bought quality food when he had enough money. He hadn't been there in quite some time. Next to it was his local bakery. A couple of minutes later, he reached Wilston Station and walked through the short tunnel that took him to the other side of the railway line. He was almost home and hosed.

While he walked, he observed everything that was happening around him. In particular, he tried to spot the car. It seemed strange his tail had abandoned the chase just because he'd decided to catch the train. But there was another possibility—one that concerned Oscar considerably because it would mean that the PI on his tail was very good at his job. It was the possibility that he'd somehow known Oscar knew he was being followed and was trying to draw him out into the open. Perhaps he'd decided that if he faked a retreat, Oscar would fall for it and walk home. Then, with Oscar off guard, all he'd have to do was track him down again.

As he reached the next intersection, he checked the lengths of both thoroughfares. A bus was approaching from the far end of Lamont Road and a painter's van was moving slowly along Abuklea Street behind him. There was still no sign of the car. He was letting his imagination run wild. Perhaps deep down inside, he'd even been hoping the chase would resume. But as

Oscar reached his house, he realised the hour for action had passed and he'd missed his chance to turn the hunter into the hunted. The time had come for a dram of whisky on the verandah.

He removed his subtle make-up and watched himself in the bathroom mirror as he transformed from Mr Newbury of the Genealogical Society back to Oscar Tremont, Investigator of the Strange and Inexplicable.

Disguising a face was one thing, but disguising a whole family and its history was a different matter altogether. Edgar was definitely on the right track—the Stayne family had surely changed its name to Taysen. It could all have been made official with the right amount of persuasion and a little knowledge about how to pull public service strings.

Oscar poured himself a dram of Lagavulin, then went out to the verandah and nestled into his thinking chair.

Jasmine Wight had given him a lot of information about the blackmailing of her family, but Oscar's next challenge was to confirm it and decide what to do with it. The coded message had mentioned some kind of proof that could condemn the Stayne family, but it gave no more information regarding the nature of the proof other than the word *Eildon*. The problem was that since the message had been written—probably almost a century ago—the houses of the families in question had been demolished and Eildon Hill itself had been transformed from a relatively natural reserve to a plateau holding a huge water reservoir. He knew his chances of locating this proof were slim.

Oscar sipped his whisky.

He didn't want to take the risk of breaking into any more houses, but it seemed he might have to do just that, unless he could locate the Wight family's lost heirlooms another way.

As the whisky took effect, he started to ask himself more questions. The first one was whether the Taysens knew about the treasure obtained by their forebears. The suspicious reaction of Helen Benison to Oscar's visit and mention of the name Stayne, as well as the fact that she or somebody else had apparently gone to the trouble of hiring a PI to tail him, indicated that she knew the Stayne family had a dark secret and that the Taysens ought to be concerned. The second question was whether the Taysens still had their forebears' tainted fruit in their possession? This was more difficult to answer. Perhaps the objects had been sold over the years. Much of it would have been used to help purchase commercial property. But there was a possibility some of the fortune was still in the hands of the Taysens. If this was indeed the case, where was it likely to be? Was it in their family home or elsewhere, like one of their properties on Queen Street or the Old Museum? This was the question Oscar had to answer. This was the key to the mystery.

13.

Edgar and Louise arrived at six forty-five that evening. They'd caught the same train. When Oscar opened the door to find their smiling faces, he knew immediately that they'd been talking about his current case. Edgar had been trying to convince Louise that Oscar was working on a real case with a paying client, but she wasn't yet fully convinced.

'Hello, what are you two doing running around together?'

'Some of us have day jobs. Still, you've had a busy one by the sound of it.'

Oscar smiled. 'Even busier than you think, Ed. A lot has happened since we spoke on the phone.'

'Other than watching the tide go out in your whisky bottle, you mean?'

'A ship sails on the ebb tide, mate. Let's go for a walk.'

'Before I give you all the details I've found out about the Taysen family, how about you explain what you've been up to today?'

Oscar recounted the day's strange events, from the moment he put his disguise on until he lost his tail at Windsor Station. Then, as they reached the end of Dover Street and turned right, Oscar moved on to the second part of his day, the events of which weren't so peculiar as the first, but equally exciting and informative.

'I decided to look into the Stayne family's properties around Brisbane, starting with the Old Museum.'

Edgar nodded. The Old Museum was a remarkable building whose singular architecture inspired mystery and stoked the imagination. It was impossible to believe that it didn't hide a secret or two.

'I found a very helpful man by the name of Michael Dolan. He was more than happy to answer my questions.'

'Did you speak to him under the guise of Mr Newbury?'

'No,' Oscar grinned. 'I went as myself.'

Edgar frowned. 'Aren't you worried that word might get back to the Taysens?'

'On the contrary, I've decided it's about time I let them know I'm investigating the Stayne family. I need to get a reaction out of them.'

'This Michael Dolan, did he tell you anything interesting?'

'Very interesting. He told me a wealthy young Richard F. Stayne had a great deal of influence over the construction of the Exhibition Building, as the Old Museum was originally known. He convinced the architect, George Addison, to have secret compartments built.'

'Remarkable! And these rooms still exist?'

'He couldn't tell me.'

'Oscar, do you think this Michael Dolan will tell the Taysens about your visit?'

'You're assuming he knows them. I hope he does. If they know I'm trying to find their family's treasure and I get a reaction out of them, it could help me answer two of my biggest questions.'

'Which are?'

'Do the Taysens know about the Wight family treasure, and if so, is it in their possession or have they too been trying to locate it?'

'In which case, you are effectively challenging them to a race.'

'Precisely,' Oscar agreed. 'A treasure hunt!'

'But how are you going to find these hidden rooms in the Old Museum? You don't even know if they exist.'

'I'm going to have to do some snooping.'

'Without being noticed?' Edgar asked, raising his eyebrows.

'You're a man about town.'

'I suppose I am. So?'

'You didn't happen to notice the upcoming events at the Old Museum?'

'I think I read about some kind of charity event.'

'Details, Edgar—what do you remember?'

'A morning tea to raise funds—' Edgar cut himself short and started to grin.

Oscar shot his friend a cheeky wink. 'I'm going to enjoy tea and scones in the museum gardens, and it's all for a worthy cause.'

14.

The morning tea had been organised to raise funds for the victims of the recent flood that had inundated parts of the city, and it only cost ten dollars for unlimited tea or coffee and pumpkin scones with strawberry jam and cream or butter. Dozens of retired people were there, like the spinsters, Susan and Daisy Latham. They'd lived their lives giggling together and attending as many social events as possible. There was also Henry Collins, a former public servant and active campaigner for the Heritage Society in its struggle to protect Brisbane's remaining historic sites. Johann and Hans Brahms, who had come to Australia from their homeland in Germany thirty years ago, were there with their wives. There were well over sixty people at the morning tea, not a bad number for a weekday.

Mr Dolan was at the museum too, but he wasn't in the garden enjoying a cup of tea. He was in his office with the door closed, talking to Nathan Taysen on the telephone.

'There's no sign of your investigator, Nathan.'

Mr Dolan listened.

'Yes, of course, but I don't think he'll be able to find the hidden rooms either. How can he expect to discover in a few days what you've been spending years researching?'

He listened.

'I know he's clever. I'm just worried that he might be *too* clever. He might work out we're using him and manage to sneak it away from right under our noses.'

Mr Dolan frowned.

'If he shows up, I'll call you. Is Grant still following him?'

He nodded and took a deep breath.

'Good. Everything's going to plan for the moment. We'll

keep in touch. Talk to you soon.'

He hung up and looked out his office window. People were busy drinking tea and chatting or wandering casually around the grounds. There were grey-haired women in floral dresses, retired men leaning on walking sticks, and the odd younger person here and there. But Oscar Tremont—of him there was no sign at all.

15.

Oscar had no trouble losing his tail. As he crossed the pedestrian bridge spanning Enoggera Creek, he heard the car speed away. It was heading back towards Newmarket Road. The man was an amateur. There was no doubt about that. He would race along Bowen Bridge Road and then turn right onto Butterfield Street in an attempt to get back on Oscar's trail on the other side of the creek. Little did he know that Oscar would have disappeared by the time he reached the other side, transforming into an elderly man wearing a white straw hat, green jumper, and beige corduroy trousers, and using a walking stick. But Oscar knew that even the most ingenious disguise was only as successful as its wearer's behaviour. He would have to alter every aspect of his person in order to be convincing, starting with his pace. He always made a note of observing people who used a walking stick, walking frame, or wheelchair.

But the car didn't come back. Oscar's tail must have decided it was safe to assume he was heading towards the Old Museum. That was a fair enough assumption after all, but he was bound to regret his slackness. He would arrive at the museum well before his target and realise after an hour of waiting for the young detective to arrive that he'd made a royal mistake.

Mr Percy Falstaff arrived at the Old Museum to find a hive of activity. It was perfect. He wanted to get inside the museum as quickly as possible but knew that such a rash move would be suspicious. He would have to pay the fee, drink a cup of tea—black, unfortunately—and strike up a conversation with a couple of other people before making a move. Mr Falstaff walked towards the main table where a money box sat waiting for him. As he moved, the carefree expression on his face camouflaged the careful attention he was paying to the way he limped and used his walking stick. Once he'd reached the table, he put his weight on the walking stick while a wrinkled right hand reached into his trouser pocket and withdrew a brown leather wallet.

'Good morning,' a young woman greeted him.

'Good morning, dear.' His voice crackled just enough to sound as though it matched Mr Falstaff's body. 'How much is it for the morning tea?'

'That's ten dollars for as much tea and scones as you like.'

'That's lovely, dear. Not too expensive for a poor old pensioner like me, and it's for a good cause too, isn't it?'

She smiled at him warmly and nodded. Oscar never failed to notice, on the rare occasions when he dressed up as an old man, that women always treated older men with a kind of special attention that younger men weren't granted so easily. Perhaps it was because they were less suspicious of the intentions of men old enough to be their grandfathers. Oscar wondered whether they were right about that, but there was no way of knowing. He could disguise himself as an older man, act like one and talk like one, but it wasn't so easy to figure out how to actually think like one.

Mr Falstaff fumbled to insert two five dollar notes into the money box while the woman poured him a cup of tea.

'White?'

'Yes, please. No sugar.'

She handed him the cup of tea.

'Thank you, dear.'

He slowly swivelled around like a failed circus performer—one hand holding the teacup and the other pushing against the walking stick. He scanned the scene with the eager attention of a bird of prey but he wore a benevolent smile. His first objective was to engage someone in conversation and to introduce himself. Nothing was more suspicious than a lone wolf at a tea party. He would allow himself five to ten minutes of mingling before going for a stroll around the Old Museum. It was only natural for a visitor to admire the remarkable building. Oscar knew the layout by heart, because the previous day he'd studied plans made available to the public on the internet. Disguised as Mr Percy Falstaff, he could pretend to be rediscovering the building for the first time in years. But getting inside would be another matter altogether. If he was the only person walking around inside the Old Museum, he would immediately arouse suspicion. He hadn't yet seen the man who had been tailing him, or even Mr Dolan for that matter, but he was sure they were nearby.

Susan and Daisy Latham were wandering through the garden looking for somebody to have a chat with. Oscar had a feeling that if he started speaking to the spinsters, he would have a hard time getting away from them afterwards. They appeared to be the kind of women who could talk for hours once they'd caught hold of a willing ear. On the upside, they would probably be so eager to talk about themselves that they wouldn't pose too many prying questions. At any rate, they'd sensed his desire to chat with someone and were being drawn to him like bees to a flower. It was too late to escape.

#

Michael Dolan went for a walk around the building, inspecting its turrets and windows as though expecting to find a cat burglar scaling it. He knew very well that Oscar was more likely to be wearing a disguise, after all, his Mr Newbury outfit had so convincingly fooled his tail, but he wanted to cover all possibilities.

After a full tour around the museum, with no sign of movement other than that of a few scavenging ibises looking for anything remotely edible, Mr Dolan found himself in the garden with the tea party guests. He examined each one closely, trying to distinguish any details that seemed incongruous. But with close to sixty people in the garden and more arriving all the time, it was a difficult task.

It was then that the stroke of good luck Oscar had been hoping for happened. Experience had taught him that good luck was only as useful as one's ability to take advantage of it, and this was an opportunity he wasn't going to let slip by.

Michael Dolan's mobile had rung, and after answering it, he'd walked away towards the grand gates that led from the museum grounds to Gregory Terrace. Oscar had no idea how long he would be away or who had called him, but he guessed he had at least a few minutes to get inside the museum and try to find a clue.

He apologised to the spinsters and hobbled towards the door to the museum.

Before stepping inside, he looked back to see Mr Dolan getting into the car that had been used to follow him. The car sped off. The stroke of good luck was bigger than he could have hoped for, so much so that he felt suspicious. Nevertheless, he wasn't about to turn back now. He stepped into the darkness of the museum and walked quickly towards the centre of the T-shaped building. His first stop would be Mr Dolan's office.

He looked up at the mezzanine to make sure nobody was watching from above.

There wasn't a soul.

He disappeared into Mr Dolan's office and knelt down at the filing cabinet. It was unlocked. He looked around as though he could smell a fishy odour in the air. It all seemed a little too easy. As he went through Mr Dolan's papers, he made sure he kept his walking stick within easy reach. If this was a trap, this part of his disguise would come in handy as a weapon.

The files were neatly arranged, and one section caught his attention immediately. He flicked through them with the dexterity of a man whose hands had not yet been wearied by age, and then all of a sudden, they stopped. A shiver ran through his body. Mr Dolan had a key clue in his possession, filed under the section that was humbly entitled 'Possible Clues'. Oscar felt like laughing, but didn't want to risk any unnecessary noise. The yellowed sheet of paper contained a message written in the same code that had been used for the message in the book at *Archives*.

Xy afuls dn mbycc oeeucnp hvyp vuc lrnls lvuqyc dvy dhyrzdv vnfb.

16.

Oscar tried to recall the substitution code, but it was no mean feat, even for him, and to make matters worse, footsteps were echoing through the hall. There was nowhere to hide in the office, and the window—which overlooked the garden—was hardly a viable option. He could just imagine the sixty or more guests in attendance staring in disbelief as an elderly man with a walking stick climbed out the window like a boy playing hide-and-seek.

He had to act fast.

He shoved the sheet of paper into a pocket, and hugging the wall, slipped out of the office. He ventured further along until he found a shallow recess housing a fire extinguisher and drew himself into it like a threatened tortoise.

The footsteps grew louder, then came to a halt at the door to the office. Several long seconds passed before they started again, slowly growing fainter.

It was a risk, but Oscar had to know. He peeped around the corner, and even from behind, he recognised the man instantly. It was the private eye who had been shadowing him.

He sank back into the recess and took the sheet of paper from his pocket. He read it again and managed to decode the message. His eyes snapped open and his grizzled moustache twitched mischievously. In his mind, he ran through all the research he'd done. Then he checked the time on his pocket watch; four minutes to noon.

Four minutes!

He dropped the charade and raced up to the mezzanine with light-footed ease, his walking stick resting on his shoulder like a rapier. He continued towards the front of the building, took a short flight of stairs to the right, and stopped at a simple wooden door. According to the plans he'd found online, it was the door to the western turret, in which George Addison's longcase clock had been placed upon completion of his architectural gem.

He crossed his fingers and reached for the doorknob, then breathed a sigh of relief when the door yielded. After another short flight of stairs, he found himself in the small turret. He dashed over to the clock to scrutinise it.

The workmanship was magnificent, in keeping with Addison's high standards. The wood was mahogany and the Roman numerals remained clear on the white enamel dial. Most impressive of all—it kept perfect time. But what caught his attention was the small brass plaque bearing the name of the clock's creator. It was positioned near the base on the left-hand side—conspicuously inconspicuous.

Be quick to press Addison when his clock chimes the twelfth hour.

Oscar felt a chill of excitement as the chiming began. After all these years, could the ingenious mechanism still work, and even if it did, would the treasure still be there in that hidden compartment that legend had expanded into a room?

He held his breath and pressed the plaque.

17.

That night, while Oscar, Louise, and Edgar were in the middle of dinner, there was a knock at the door.

'Who could that be, honey?'

Oscar didn't reply, but he shot Edgar a wary glance.

'Oscar?' she asked nervously.

'Wait here, Louise. Edgar, come with me.'

Edgar placed his knife and fork on his plate and stood slowly, mentally preparing himself. His gaze lingered on the knife.

'Be careful!' Louise whispered.

They nodded and walked towards the front door, Oscar leading the way. Before reaching it, he raised his scarred right hand, bringing Edgar to a halt. He then slipped into his bedroom and peeked out through the blinds in an attempt to identify the unexpected visitor. But it was too dark outside. He could only see two obscure shapes waiting at the door. One of them knocked again.

Oscar turned to Edgar, who was waiting at the bedroom door, and made a quick downwards motion with his finger. Edgar understood and switched the verandah light on. All of a sudden, the dark shapes became distinguishable. One of them was the man Oscar had been followed by. The other was a stranger.

He grabbed his walking stick and walked over to the front door, giving Edgar a look that meant *get ready for some action*.

He pulled the door open.

'Mr Tremont?' the stranger asked, his fake smile disguising the scowl Oscar had seen through the window.

'That's right. I've crossed paths with your friend, but I don't have the honour of his name, or yours.'

'My name is Nathan Taysen, and this is my brother, Grant. We just want to have a talk.'

He wasn't a private eye after all. He was a member of the family. Oscar pretended not to be surprised.

'A talk?'

'Please, hear us out.'

'We can talk out here on the verandah if you don't mind, gentlemen.'

They nodded.

'Do excuse my lack of usual hospitality.'

'Not at all. We understand. Mr Tremont, we believe you have found a treasure belonging to our family.'

Oscar thought before replying, but made sure not to hesitate too long.

'Well, I certainly am looking for a treasure, but it's one that belongs to another family, not the Taysens or the Staynes. But I can't imagine why you think I've found it.'

The brothers looked at each other.

'It's just a suspicion, Mr Tremont.'

'I can understand that. I'm also a suspicious person. Let me ask you a question. If a man of principle found a treasure that had been obtained through immoral means several generations back and it was suddenly within his powers to hand it over to the rightful owners, what would you expect him to do?'

Nathan Taysen grinned. 'It's not a matter of what you think is right. It's a matter of the law.'

'Indeed. Then the question is whether can you provide concrete evidence indicating that the treasure we are seeking belongs—legally speaking—to your family.'

They didn't respond at first.

'Let me just say that if you were to find the treasure, we would like to have the opportunity to inspect it.'

'Duly noted,' Oscar replied.

'We won't bother you any longer,' Nathan said. 'Good night.'

'Good night.'

As Oscar closed the door, he wondered whether Nathan had been telling the truth when he said they wouldn't bother him any longer. Probably not, he decided. After all, *he* hadn't told *them* the truth.

'What are we going to do now?' Edgar asked.

'We're going to do nothing whatsoever. This game is over.

If they try to keep tabs on me, I'll throw them off track so they think I've given up. In the meantime, I'm going to give you a token of my gratitude and I'm going to take my fee. Then I'll go and pay the Wight family a discreet visit. After that, I'll come back home and spend some time with my darling wife. I don't always appreciate how patient she is with me.'

'No, you don't,' Edgar agreed. 'Don't worry about a token of appreciation for me. I know you appreciate my help. I'm just glad to be a part of the adventure. I'm going home for some sleep. Call me if you get yourself into any more trouble.'

'Thanks, Edgar, but I think everything will be all right now.'

Edgar went inside to bid Louise a good evening before leaving. As soon as he'd gone, Oscar told her he would be out for an hour or so and would explain everything when he returned. He went under the house without turning the light on and felt his way towards the safe where he kept the clandestine tools of his trade and where at present could be found a small polished wooden box that now contained the bounty of a once prestigious family. He removed it from the safe and placed it in a black backpack. Then, with the stealth of a cloud across a moonless sky, he began his jog through the streets of Wilston, up to the Wight family home.

18.

'Hello?'

'Hello, Mr Wight. Do you have a minute?'

'That depends. I'm not used to visitors this late at night. Who are you and what's this about?'

'It's a long story, but to cut to the chase, Mr Wight, I've discovered your family's treasure.'

Eamon was speechless. He just stared at Oscar.

'The Wight family treasure. I've found it.'

'How? It's been missing for generations.'

'As I said, it's a long story. I'm going to have to start from the beginning. Can I come in?'

'Ah, it's not a good time.'

'Jasmine's feeling unwell?'

Eamon's jaw dropped.

'I need to speak to you about her. Do you understand? This can't go on. She needs professional help.'

'How—?'

'Hold on a minute,' Oscar said. 'Listen to me. I must insist on this point. Before I show you what's in this bag, I need your word that you'll get Jasmine the help she needs.'

Eamon drew a deep breath.

'We'll do this together,' Oscar said more softly now. 'I don't question your love as a father, but you're not equipped to deal with her condition. She'll only get better if she has proper treatment.'

Eamon rubbed his face with both hands as though waking himself from a bad dream.

'So?'

For a moment, Oscar was worried he might be stubborn enough to refuse and tell him to keep the treasure and be on his way.

He didn't.

'Very well, Mr—?'

'Tremont—Oscar Tremont, Investigator of the Strange and Inexplicable.'

'I accept your terms.' He paused. 'And I thank you from the bottom of my heart. You'd better come inside.'

#

'I'm sorry I was distant over the past few days, honey, but it was a big case,' Oscar told Louise when he got home.

'You can make up for it by spending time with me now and telling me all about it.'

'That's exactly what I intend to do.'

'Will you be paid adequately for the case?'

Oscar smiled and grabbed his wife gently but firmly by the arm. He spun her around until she had her back to him.

'What are you doing?'

Oscar slipped something cold and smooth around her neck and led her to the bathroom so she could look in the mirror.

'I've already paid myself sufficiently handsomely, and I've kept a little souvenir of the mystery for you,' he answered.

'*Magnifique!* They look like real rubies.'

'*C'est le cas, mon amour,*' he whispered.

She kissed him. 'How did you get this?'

'It's a long story and you won't approve of parts of it, but I'll tell you everything. Let's make ourselves comfortable before I begin.'

He led her to the sofa.

She curled up at one end and wrapped her arms around her knees. 'I'm ready,' she told him.

'Well, it all started at *Archives Fine Books*.'

The Ghosts of Walhalla

1.

'Do you know what I'd like to do to celebrate?' Louise asked, snuggling up next to her husband on the sofa.

She was right. It was an occasion that deserved to be marked. The case of the Stayne fortune had been challenging and nerve-wracking, but also financially rewarding. At present, the investigator of strange occurrences found himself in the unusual position of not having to worry about paying the rent on time and being able to stock their home with such basic necessities as a bottle of decent whisky.

'Tell me. What would you like to do?'

'You know I need a break from work, and that I haven't seen Jessica in ages.'

'Jessica?' Oscar tried to put a face to the name.

'You've probably forgotten her. That's how long it's been.'

'She's your friend in Melbourne, isn't she?'

Louise nodded suggestively.

'You're saying you want a holiday in Melbourne?'

'Spot on, Sherlock.'

'Sounds good to me. I can't remember the last time I went there. As a matter of fact, there's a secluded little spot in Victoria that I'd like to visit. I've been meaning to go there for years, and it isn't far from the city.'

Louise smiled knowingly. 'Would it happen to be a weird place teeming with mystery and local legends?'

'Do you know where I'm talking about?' he led her on.

'Not at all. I just know my husband.'

'Well, I suppose you've just about summed it up. It's practically a ghost town these days, with a population of about twenty, but it had thousands living there back in the days of the gold rush.'

'A ghost town,' Louise mused. She had a cheeky glint in her eye. 'It must be haunted.'

'So they say, but you know I'm not easily sold on tales of ghosts and ghouls.'

'You're a rational man who's obsessed with the irrational.'

Oscar didn't reply. She'd probably hit the nail on the head. It was true that all things illogical and incongruous fascinated him. He was always seeking to convince himself that no mystery stemmed from a cause that the methodical application of reason could not unearth.

'Does it have a supposedly haunted pub for us to stay in?'

'I don't know about that, but it probably has a free camping area nearby. I'll check it out if you're interested.'

'Let me get this straight, *chéri*. You want to celebrate your big success by camping for free?'

He frowned at her, wondering what she thought was so strange about that. Then he nodded.

Louise leaned over and kissed him. That was one of the reasons she loved him so much. In some ways, he was a complicated man, always ready for a puzzle to solve or a mystery to ponder. But on the other hand, he was one of the most down-to-earth people she'd ever met. He knew how to enjoy the simple pleasures in life.

'It's a lovely idea. I can't remember the last time we went

camping.'

Neither could Oscar.

2.

The road through the dense forest was winding and narrow, and every now and then, Oscar had to steer around a fallen rock or dead branch that blocked their way. The rental car handled much better than his own, which was back in Brisbane, parked outside his Dover Street cottage.

They'd enjoyed their time in Melbourne. Louise had gone to the Victoria Markets and bought a pair of earrings and then taken Oscar to several galleries where he'd watched her stroll in admiration along walls displaying the work of some of the city's most talented photographers. Oscar had enjoyed the images for the stories they told and the questions they posed, as did his wife. But as a budding photographer, Louise also understood the technical brilliance behind them. She could analyse the way light and darkness had been contrasted and knew without reading the details of each shot what kind of lens the photographer had used. Oscar was impressed by his wife's skills of deduction in her chosen art.

Jessica had given them a guided tour of the city. They'd stopped for a beer at a handful of historic pubs, and visited the Old Melbourne Gaol, where Ned Kelly had been hanged after his failed attempt to create a republic in the middle of Queen Victoria's colony. But a few days in the city had been enough, and Oscar was now very much looking forward to their next destination. He hoped it would be every bit as interesting as he imagined.

As the car weaved its way along the road, he glanced at Louise. It was thanks to her that they were there. He often needed her to tell him what to do and remind him that they both deserved an occasional treat. He looked back at the road, not daring to take his attention away from the curves, rocky embankments, and potholes for more than an instant.

'Mind if I put some music on?' Louise asked.

'Not at all.' He quickly glanced at her again and her new earrings bounced as they hit a bump in the road.

'*Doucement!*' she complained, instinctively using French.

'Sorry, honey, but if I'd swerved around that particular bump, we'd be at the bottom of the gully by now.'

She frowned as she looked out her window and down the steep slope, then flicked through her iPhone playlist and chose the acoustic ballads of Passenger over the chick rock of The Jezebels.

As the first song started, they arrived at a bridge spanning a deep ravine. At the bottom, Stringers Creek flowed through a maze of rocks. Crossing the bridge, Oscar noticed a lower and much older railway bridge to their right.

They passed the Walhalla Railway Station and the charming log cabin with a wooden shingle roof that hung to the mountainside, then just around the next bend, they found tombstones leaning at awkward angles, clinging to the slope.

The road continued uphill, following Stringers Creek, the waters of which had first betrayed the presence of alluvial gold one fateful day about one hundred and fifty years earlier. It was one of the explorers, a Swede who'd been lured by the glint of the heavenly element, who'd given Walhalla its name.

'It's gorgeous here,' Louise remarked as they passed the old post office and general store, both of which were closed. 'Look at the fire station. It's built across the creek like a bridge.'

Driving slowly, Oscar admired the charming buildings of the ghost town. Groups of school children doing a historical treasure hunt confirmed that they were not alone in Walhalla. Oscar drove even more slowly as they stood to either side of the narrow road to let him pass. They then hurried along in search of the answer to the next question on their worksheet.

It seemed that quite a number of buildings were still in service, but The Greyhorse Café was the only one that was open for business at that particular moment, and Oscar saw two teachers placing an order at the counter.

The scattered houses that lay to the left of the road, across the narrow ditch through which Stringers Creek flowed, or on higher ground to the right, were either abandoned and rundown, beautifully maintained and in use as private homes, or serving as guesthouses. Even of the two latter kinds, many were clearly unoccupied. Vacancy signs with telephone numbers were abundant. Oscar had noticed there was no mobile signal in the valley, but there was a red phone booth near the post office. Prospective guests would have to make calls from there.

'Where's the campsite?' Louise asked.

'It's supposed to be at the end of the road, about two kilometres north of the post office,' Oscar replied.

'We must almost be there then.'

To their left, across the creek, an enormous mass of grey rubble rose, leaning against the mountainside. The carcasses of rusted machinery on top and the sign hanging at the entrance to the wooden bridge down by the road confirmed what Oscar had suspected. It was the Long Tunnel Extended Mine; the only of the town's numerous mineshafts open to the public.

'It reminds me of the kind of ghost town you'd find in an episode of Scooby-Doo,' Louise observed.

'You read my mind. I wonder if there's a bogeyman lurking in the abandoned mine.'

'If there is, Oscar Tremont will catch him and reveal his true identity.' She laughed. 'It will be the park ranger, I reckon.'

'Do you indeed?'

'I bet you London to a block.'

'London to a *brick*, my lovely froggy. But our most immediate challenge is to work out how to put the tent up. We don't have a Mystery Machine to sleep in like Scooby and the gang.'

They laughed.

'No, but we should get one,' Louise said, a hint of mischief in her voice.

Oscar bit his bottom lip and nodded slowly.

'We really should.'

3.

The camping area consisted of a short bridge with white corner posts that stretched over a steep shelf in the creek and an unsealed parking area that was separated from a lush camping ground by a row of low, half-rotten wooden barriers. A stone shelter with a corrugated iron roof and a gas tank attached at the back provided campers with a simple kitchen. Behind this building, to the north, the land rose in a heavily forested slope through which a track called the Tramline Walkway penetrated. According to the sign at its entrance, the track curved around the western side of the camping area and then headed south along the side of the mountains that overlooked Walhalla.

There were toilets housed in another simple stone structure and over by the creek were three picnic tables standing at an equal distance from each other. From these tables, the sparkling water could be admired as it rushed downhill over the rocky creek bed.

It was a pretty area, and one they were going to have all to themselves. There wasn't a single campervan in the car park or tent pitched on the grass.

Louise was the first to voice her thoughts.

'You don't think it's strange nobody else is staying here? After all, this has to be one of the most picturesque townships in the whole country, and we're only a two-hour drive from Melbourne.'

'I guess so, but it doesn't matter, does it? We can spend some quality time together—no friends, no schedule, no work.'

'You're right. No cases for you to take on or boss for me to put up with.'

Louise looked around. Apart from some freshly charred wood piled up in a makeshift bonfire, there was no sign that anybody had camped there in quite some time. Oscar was more precise in his study of the campsite. Judging by the faded colour and stunted growth of a couple of rectangular patches of grass, and estimating the rate of growth for the time of year and weather conditions, which had been ominous since arriving in Victoria, he estimated that the last tent pitched there had been about a week ago, and for a period of about two days—so, presumably, last weekend. Later, during his first visit to the men's toilets, he would find further and far less pleasant evidence to confirm his estimation.

'Where do you think we should put our tent up?' Louise asked.

'How about in the corner over there,' he suggested, pointing to the south, where a waist-high wooden retaining wall separated the open campground from higher land where birds were frolicking in the trees and bushes. Not far away, to the west, was the toilet block, and to the east a picnic table nestled amongst bushy trees at the verge of the embankment leading down to the narrow creek.

'Perfect,' she agreed. 'Let's get the car unpacked before it starts to rain.'

It only took about a quarter of an hour to pitch the tent, much to their surprise.

'Just in time!' Louise shouted as the grey clouds that had been hanging menacingly around the mountain peaks moved down into the valley. Rain pelted down with angry force.

The frolicking birds became hysterical, and Oscar and Louise dived into the tent and zipped it closed. After making sure no water was seeping in, they took advantage of the lousy weather to enjoy each other's company for an hour.

By the time the clouds had emptied themselves, the sun was sinking behind the treetops on the mountain behind the toilet block. Its pink smile lit up the humid sky and reminded them that they really ought to prepare their dinner before it got too dark. They both wanted to have a warm shower before eating, but free camping areas didn't include such luxuries. They settled for a warm bowl of pumpkin soup with bread and butter instead, followed by a bottle of pinot noir.

'Look what I have here,' Louise announced, pulling a pack of cards from her overnight bag.

'You wouldn't rather play chess?'

'No, I would not,' she replied firmly.

Louise spent the next hour winning a variety of card games until her eyelids grew heavy and she decided it was time for bed, much to her husband's relief.

#

The low rumble of an engine woke Oscar in the middle of the night. The sound smothered the soothing rustle of the creek that had lulled him to sleep. He couldn't see out of the tent but could tell that the vehicle was bigger than a car and that the headlights weren't on, because there wasn't even the slightest glow playing on the thin walls of the tent.

He wondered why anybody would be driving up a dark, winding country road without lights on. He could feel the strings of curiosity tugging at his still dormant mind. He also needed to relieve his bladder. The two urges combined were more than he could bear, so he crawled out into the cool night air.

But it was too late. The van was already heading down the road and all he noticed was that whenever the brakes were applied, only one brake light came on.

He slipped around the side of the tent and relieved himself. Once he'd finished, he looked all around, but he couldn't see anything except the dull glow of the overcast night sky. Nothing stirred in the campsite or the mountains around it.

Oscar didn't believe in ghosts. He always told himself there was a rational explanation to every mystery. Yet somehow, standing there half-awake in the darkness of that valley, a hidden world where thousands had lived and died so many years ago, and where now only a handful of permanent residents occupied a few quaint and quirky edifices, he had to wonder.

He shivered and took refuge in the tent.

4.

Bright sunshine and the raucous laughter of kookaburras chased any thoughts of ghosts from Oscar's mind as he opened his eyes. Louise was fast asleep, and he knew that if he woke her up before she was ready, he'd regret it. Instead, he remained wrapped up in his sleeping bag and started to think about how they could spend the day.

Louise would want to drink a coffee at the café just down the road. After that, they could explore the township on foot, and he would be able to study its history while Louise took photos.

He closed his eyes again and managed to sleep for a while longer, until Louise stirred from her slumber. Then, when she was almost awake, he crawled out of the tent and prepared a simple breakfast of Weetbix with milk, honey, and sultanas.

#

The young woman who ran The Greyhorse had a figure that was almost as curvy as the road to Walhalla. Oscar noticed that about her immediately, and Louise noticed that he'd noticed. She wore no wedding ring, or any other jewellery for that matter. She was dressed plainly in a tight black T-shirt that did her tits all the justice they deserved and a flowing violet skirt whose embroidered hem licked at her black leather boots when she walked.

'You're staying here in Walhalla?' she asked with a casual smile while she worked the coffee machine with expert hands.

'We're camping just up the road here,' Louise answered. 'Ours is the only tent there.'

She could tell by Louise's tone that she was a little concerned about the lack of campers, as though there had to be some sinister reason.

'Oh, that's normal. It's only Thursday today. You can expect some company over the weekend. Where are you from?'

'Brisbane,' Oscar told her. 'And my wife is from France originally.'

She winked at him, as though to imply there was something intrinsically kinky about being married to a French woman.

'*Enchantée*,' she said to Louise. 'My name's Fay.'

'I'm Oscar.'

'Louise.'

'Nice to meet you. How long are you staying?'

They looked at each other. 'We're not sure just yet,' Louise said. 'A couple of nights most likely.'

'Or maybe for ever,' Fay laughed. 'That's what happened to me.'

'Really, tell us about it,' Louise said.

'I will, but I should warn you, once you get me talking, I never shut up.'

'Louise is exactly the same.'

She elbowed him in the side.

'Grab a table and I'll join you once your coffees are ready.'

They chose a table in the sun. There was nobody else around at all. It was still too early for day visitors. The bandstand, an elevated structure made of skilfully worked wood, stood across the road and creek from them. A little further up the hill was a building with a plaque bearing the words "Walhalla Masonic Lodge, No. 69". A path that led between the bandstand and the lodge, and then became a set of stairs, joined the Tramline Walkway further up the side of the mountain. Oscar told himself they ought to follow that track back to the camping area later on. It would give Louise the opportunity to take some great photos of the township.

Fay brought their coffees out and sat down at the table with them, rather close to Oscar.

'As I was saying, I came here with my sister four years ago. It was supposed to be a girly getaway, if you know what I mean. No men allowed!' She gave Oscar an admonishing glance, as though he'd done something wrong on behalf of his entire gender—but then she winked at him.

He shifted uneasily in his seat and looked across at Louise to read on her face the confirmation of what he suspected; that Fay was flirting with him right under his wife's nose. Louise's lips were pursed in an attempt to stop herself from laughing. As long as she didn't go too far and Oscar didn't flirt back, everything would be fine.

'Let me guess,' Louise volunteered, breaking the silence. 'A boy came along.'

'Of course,' Fay replied. 'We got along just fine in the beginning, and after a few months, I moved in with him. But then, the relationship turned sour. As it turned out, I wasn't the only weekender he'd been showing the sights.'

'Men!' Louise groaned, shaking her head.

Oscar looked at her blankly.

'Anyway, he decided to leave Walhalla, and I wanted to stay. So, I took over the lease of his cottage and kept my job here at the café, and, well, here I've stayed.'

'Are you happy here?' Louise asked.

'Yes and no. Most of the locals get along like a house on fire, with a few exceptions. The only thing is, I haven't had much luck in the romance department.'

Louise was about to continue asking questions when a man stumbled around the corner behind them, walking loudly and clumsily. He was middle-aged and wearing strange clothes; a pair of fluorescent orange shorts and white socks with sandals. In each hand was a plastic shopping bag full of books.

'Oh, here comes Ben. I'll explain later,' Fay whispered.

He walked up to Oscar, ignoring the women, and stared at him with blatant curiosity. He raised his bags and shouted, 'Books!'

'Sorry?' Oscar asked.

'Books?' he repeated the word as a question, slightly less loudly. 'You want books?'

Oscar wasn't sure whether the man wanted to sell them or simply give them away, but either way, he wasn't interested.

'No. I have a whole stack I haven't read yet, thank you.'

Ben just looked at him for a few long seconds.

'Encyclopaedias!' he shouted.

'Thanks, but no thanks.'

Ben frowned and sighed loudly, as though he were the one trying to talk to a simpleton. Then, without another word, he stomped downhill, mumbling to himself as he went.

'That's Ben. He's Helen Fordyce's son. He's a bit, well, I'm sure you noticed. Helen and Ben live at Spetts Cottage. You must have seen it on the way down from the camping area. It's a gorgeous cottage. They live off her husband's inheritance, and she spends most of her time looking after Ben. It's quite sad really. Ben can be annoying, always trying to hawk old books and other trinkets, but honestly, they're both lovely people.'

'I'm sure they are,' Louise said. 'I love meeting people, especially in unusual places. I don't think you can live in a town like this without being a bit of a character. I mean that in a good way, of course,' she hastened to add.

'I know exactly what you mean, and you're absolutely right. I don't think anybody in Walhalla could be described as normal.'

'Could you give us some tips about how to spend the day?' Oscar asked. 'I'm interested in taking a tour of the old mine.'

'I'm afraid you'll have to wait until the weekend for a tour. The information centre is just down the road. They'll have all the details. There are a couple of shops that should be open down that way. The lolly shop is great, especially if you want to meet an interesting character, and you also have the art and craft shop. Apart from that, and this might sound strange, but the old cemetery really gives you an insight into the Walhalla of yesteryear.'

'Why not?' Oscar said, turning to Louise. 'It could be a good spot to put your camera into action.'

'Oh, it is,' Fay agreed. 'And the best way to take photos of the town is to take the stairs up to the walking track. There are several shorter tracks branching off into the forest from there. But don't go too far. You don't want to get lost in the mountains.'

They had another coffee before heading off towards the cemetery, where the tombstones told stories of lives cut short by mishap and malady. They wandered through the resting place, taking care where they stepped both out of respect and because the terrain was steep and uneven. Oscar watched Louise as she took picture after picture, capturing the morose atmosphere of the site with her camera.

After a while, she turned to him and said, 'Let's go up to the track through the forest now. I want to take some photos of life.'

Oscar smiled. He was happy to see her inspired.

'If you're a good boy and prepare lunch while I take photos, I'll cook dinner and we can play chess instead of cards tonight.'

'You've got yourself a deal.'

5.

Oscar woke in the middle of the night again, but no rumbling motor had disturbed him from his light slumber. A less tangible reason was behind it. No more than a feeling really. It was the vague notion that he was missing out on something of interest, that Walhalla was a far more eventful place by night than it was by day. Of course, that didn't make sense. There were still no other campers sharing the grounds with them, and he had to assume that the ghost town's few inhabitants would be snuggled up in bed or sitting by the fireplace in their living rooms at that late hour. He could imagine Fay dreaming she had a man in bed with her. He could also picture Ben rummaging through his bits and pieces, wondering what he might be able to sell or trade.

He closed his eyes and listened to the creek, waiting for its constant note to lull him back to sleep.

But he no longer wanted to sleep. The need to experience Walhalla in the dark was too pressing. He didn't believe in phantoms and hauntings. He was far too rational for campfire stories of things going bump in the night or vexed lovers coming back from the grave to seek revenge. But another part of him, just as curious as his ever-questioning rational part, kept testing him. This part of Oscar wondered if he really was so sceptical. Sometimes, it seemed as though it *wanted* him to believe.

Before he'd finished thinking it through, Oscar was creeping out of the tent and into the cold dark with no more than a torch to guide him.

Instead of walking along the road and possibly attracting attention, he decided to follow the Tramline Walkway that he'd taken with Louise to return to the camping area earlier that day. He hesitated a moment to make sure he hadn't disturbed Louise while leaving the tent and walked slowly across the camping area and over to the rocky track.

It seemed so very different at night. The darkness had changed the walkway beyond recognition. He could imagine how it must have been over a century ago with noisy trolleys full of ore from the mines following the rails which had lain where he was walking.

The crunching of rocks and leaves underfoot had barely been audible during the day, but it was now disturbingly loud. He wanted to be quiet, so he tried to tread softly, even though he guessed there was nobody around.

Only, there must have been somebody, because he heard a voice.

He stopped dead in his tracks and held his breath.

No, not a voice. It was sobbing, distant and muffled. It wasn't wailing or screaming, but quiet weeping. Was that what a ghost sounded like?

A ghost? Only flesh and blood could cry.

He kept listening. There was no mistaking what he heard.

'Hello?' he whispered.

No reply. There was only sobbing as constant and unabated as the flow of the creek below.

Oscar tried to work out where the sound was coming from, but it was all around him, yet somehow distant. It was both under him and right beside him.

He continued along the track until he couldn't hear the sobbing any longer, and then, shivering, he turned on his heels and hurried back. But the sobbing had stopped. He was alone.

He remained there like a statue for several minutes until he had to ask himself if he hadn't imagined it all. But it was a question he couldn't answer.

He waited a while longer, and when the silence was more than he could cope with, he headed back to his sleeping wife.

6.

He didn't manage to sleep well the rest of that night. The directionless sobbing was still all around him, but he kept telling himself that it was impossible. What he was hearing was just the memory of the sound that had haunted him, or to be more precise, the memory of the sound that he must have imagined hearing.

In the morning, once daylight had slowly crept into the valley and the cheerful singing of bower birds, kookaburras, and rosellas had commenced, Louise finally stirred. He had to resist the urge to tell her about his nocturnal wanderings until she was fully awake. But he didn't even have to bring the subject up. Once fully awake, after a great deal of yawning and moaning, she frowned at him.

He decided to get in first. 'You woke up during the night?'

She just stared at him, and he knew he was going to have to apologise.

'Yes, I did,' she replied slowly. 'I woke up alone in a tent in an otherwise empty camping area in a supposedly haunted old mining town.'

'Hold that thought!' Oscar said excitedly.

'What thought? That I'm pissed off right now!'

He adored the way she pronounced that word *peest* in her French accent. He liked the message she was conveying a great deal less.

'No, what I mean is, hold the thought about Walhalla being haunted.'

She was still frowning.

'By the way, I'm sorry.'

She struggled to stop the frown from becoming a smile.

'So, what happened? You used your legendary skills of deduction and rational thought to prove once and for all that ghosts do not exist?' She emphasised the final four words.

It was Oscar's turn to frown.

'No, not at all. In fact...'

'In fact, what? *Quoi?*' she challenged him.

'I really do think I'm going insane.'

'Insane?' She shook her head. 'People call you eccentric and strange, some call you freaky, but not insane.'

'Who?'

'That's not the point, *chéri*. What I'm saying is, you are many things, but insane isn't one of them.'

Oscar lowered his voice, despite the fact that unless somebody was sneaking around outside their tent, nobody but Louise could have heard him. 'The thing is, I think, although I can't be sure, that I heard a ghost crying.'

'Wow!'

Her reaction wasn't what he'd been expecting.

'Wow?'

'Yes. *Wow!* You know that *I* believe in ghosts, and I don't know anybody as rational as you. So, if you heard a ghost, it can only mean that they really *do* exist.'

Oscar groaned. He couldn't argue with her reasoning.

'Unless I really *am* going insane.'

'No,' she said. 'No, no, no, I don't think you are. I'm your wife, so I would have noticed.'

He had to concur with her reasoning again, but he couldn't really have heard a ghost, could he? It was unusual for him, but Oscar didn't know what to think. What he did know was that he had to talk to the locals. If he was going to believe in ghosts, he wanted a solid reason to believe. He wanted to know what the residents of Walhalla had experienced.

'I'd like to go back to The Greyhorse and have a chat with Fay.'

Louise raised her eyebrows. 'Is this desire to have a *tête-à-tête* to do with ghosts, or something fleshier? You need to watch out for her.'

But Oscar wasn't in the mood for jokes. 'I'm serious, Louise. What happened last night gave me the creeps.'

She could tell he meant it. 'All right, we could both use a cappuccino with an extra shot. On the way, how about you show me exactly where you heard the sobbing. Women are more attuned to these kinds of vibes, you know?'

Under different circumstances, Oscar would have smiled at her choice of words, *attuned* and *vibes*. Her English was coming along in leaps and bounds and it impressed him when she used new words, especially ones he seldom uttered. Maybe she was right. Maybe he did need some female intuition to explain this particular mystery.

'That's a good idea,' he said. 'We need to have a close look at the spot in broad daylight.'

They took what they needed for the morning, making sure to grab money, hats, cameras, a notebook and pen, some water, and a pair of binoculars. Oscar was beginning to wonder whether he should have brought a Ouija board with him.

Once they had everything, they set off towards the track.

After several minutes, during which Oscar tried to recognise each bend in the track from the night before, he slowed down a little more with each step before coming to a complete halt.

He looked around and said simply, 'It was about here.'

Louise scanned the scene, peering down the tree-covered slope to her left and up the rock face to her right. She could catch a glimpse of a garden down below, a patch of neat lawn or well-tended flowerbed visible between the branches and trunks. Neither side of the track revealed a place where a person could have been sobbing, unless he or she had been perched on a tree branch or leaning against the trunks that resisted the steep slope of the mountain.

'I couldn't have heard anybody sobbing in the cottage down there,' Oscar pointed out, reading his wife's thoughts.

'No, definitely not,' she agreed. 'What's on top of the rock face there?'

He stared at his wife, and then stared up the rock face. 'I'm not a mountain goat.'

'No, you're not, but you *are* the fabulous Oscar Tremont, Investigator of the Strange and Inexplicable!' she reminded him with an encouraging smile.

He looked up again and shrugged. A little further along the track was a breach in the sheer surface of rock. Some short but sturdy trees had taken root within.

'Have you got your camera ready?'

She had indeed. If Oscar was going to slip and go rolling down onto the track, she would capture every bump and twist.

'Here goes!' He grabbed the trunk nearest him and pulled himself up. His feet slipped on the dirt, but once he had them on firm ground, he swung himself to the next tree and hung on. He was the opposite of a sloth, instead of moving from tree to tree with lethargy and ease, he was all jerks and groans. All the while, Louise was snapping away.

He made it onto the rocks and breathed deeply. Then he looked around.

There were more trees and another embankment leading even higher, not a flat clearing supporting a hidden cottage or a weathered old shack. To one side was a narrow, natural passage. It was no more than a crack between the steep embankment and a rocky knob. Oscar peered through and saw yet more bushes and another rock face beyond.

He took a deep breath and closed his eyes. No sobbing. No cold shivers. No ghostly hand on the shoulder. There was nothing haunting at all. But then again, it was the morning and the sun was up. Ghosts only appeared at dusk and during the night, didn't they?

'Oscar!'

Her voice made him jump.

'Yes! There's nothing. I'm coming back down!'

He had no idea how close he had come.

#

Fay was happy to see them again.

'Oscar and Lisa!'

'Hello, Fay. By the way, the name's Louise.'

'Oh, sorry. Good to have you back. I'll just be a minute.'

She hurried inside.

'She got your name right,' Louise remarked as they sat down.

The Greyhorse was a lot busier that morning. Two men in work clothes were sitting at one table and laughing loudly as they ate bacon and egg panini. The truck with chainsaws, fuel cans, ropes, and sundry other tools in the tray was undoubtedly theirs. A man and a woman, who appeared to be visitors, sat at another table. Both wore sunglasses and hats, even though the sun wasn't yet high in the sky.

'Oscar and Louise, two large cappuccinos, right?'

'Good memory,' Oscar congratulated her.

She smiled as she walked off.

'Good memory,' Louise mimicked him. 'Oh, and nice pair of jugs.'

The workmen must have overheard, because they burst out laughing again.

Oscar just ignored her.

Fay was back in no time with their coffees and sat down with them like they were old friends.

'Did you have a good night?'

'Yes,' Oscar replied before Louise had a chance to mention what had happened. He didn't want to let everybody in town know about his experience and could tell that a gossip like Fay wasn't the type of girl to bite her tongue.

'That's good to hear. You should have some more company tonight, being Friday,' she said for Louise's benefit.

'I hope so.'

'Walhalla is supposed to have a lot of ghost stories,' Oscar said casually. He didn't fail to notice that his words caught the attention of one of the workmen.

Fay nodded emphatically.

'Do you know any of them?'

'Of course, everybody here knows one or two. I'm by no means the local expert though. That would be Anne. She does a ghost tour every Saturday night.'

'Tomorrow night,' Oscar mused. 'We should do that.'

'Definitely,' Louise said. 'Do you know any of them, Fay?'

'Well, there's the one about Spetts Cottage. It's a spooky tale. Spetts Cottage is where Helen and Ben live. You met Ben yesterday.'

They nodded.

'I'm not sure when her late husband bought the place, but it was the Spetts family who built it back in the 1870s. There were several daughters in the family, and one of them was called Rhoda. She was due to be married one November, but something went wrong. Nobody seems to know exactly. Some say her husband stood her up. Every now and then, in the month of November, people report seeing a woman in a wedding gown standing in one corner of the garden.'

'It's November now,' Louise pointed out, and her face seemed a little paler than usual.

'Do people hear her speaking, or crying?' Oscar asked.

'No, they just see her figure.'

'And she's always in the garden of Spetts Cottage?'

'According to the story.'

'Nobody has ever spotted her around town?'

'No,' Fay answered firmly, and Oscar realised that his questions were starting to make her feel nervous.

'Just one more question. Has Helen or Ben ever seen her?'

'I don't know about Ben. You can't get much sense out of him, but Helen has seen Rhoda.'

Oscar frowned. It didn't seem to be Rhoda then. He'd heard crying, and it was up on the track. Was there another ghost in Walhalla? Why not, after all? He drank his cappuccino before it got too cold.

'You know who else can tell you some ghost stories?' Fay went on. 'The druid.'

'The druid?' Louise asked.

'A druid is a Celtic priest.'

'I know what it means. It's pretty much the same word in French. Are you saying there's one here in Walhalla?'

'Well, his name is Donald, and nobody much talks to him. He lives in a caravan up near the old hospital. He's really weird and is into spirits and herbs and all that sort of thing. I'm open to all that, but he's just a strange hermit. He never comes down here for a coffee. As a matter of fact, I'm not even sure if he uses money. He lives in his own world. So, we call him the druid.'

'He sounds interesting,' Oscar said. 'Is he friendly?'

Fay didn't know what to say. 'Well, he's neither friendly nor unfriendly. I don't really know him, you see. He's a hermit. He's obsessed with ghosts though. Anne talks to him sometimes. If you tell him you want to know about haunted sites in Walhalla, he might tell you what he knows.'

7.

Oscar and Louise found a booklet about ghosts on sale for three dollars at the information centre. They also booked themselves on the ghost tour for Saturday night.

'You'll love it,' said the clerk, who was called Les Gilchrest according to his name tag. He was a tall man with thinning red hair and a bushy beard to match. His face was jovial, but there was a hawkish keenness to his blue eyes. 'Anne's tour is among the finest ghost tours in all of Australia. She knows her history, official and unofficial, and never stops doing research and collecting articles and books on Walhalla. More importantly though, her tour is a lot of fun, and *very* creepy!'

'I'm looking forward to it,' Oscar replied. 'What parts of town does the tour go through?'

'Every tour is different. Walhalla is so haunted that Anne can't possibly take you past the scene of every reported ghost sighting in town in one evening. But you can be sure you'll hear a few chilling tales about Windsor House. Is that where you're staying?'

'We're camping.'

'Right, well, I don't want to steal Anne's thunder, but Windsor House will be on the tour. She'll also take you up past

Spetts Cottage, around to the old school building, and up to the entrance to the Extended Long Tunnel Mine. She won't take you all the way up to the old hospital, because it's out of bounds at the moment, but she'll probably mention it. As I say though,' Les repeated clearly so as to rule out the possibility of any misunderstanding, 'every tour is a slight variation on the last. We try to mix it up a little.'

'That sounds great. There are no ghost stories about the camping area or the stretch of the Tramline Walkway leading off from it?' Oscar asked, adding a casual laugh.

Les paused for a while, sorting through the dozens of ghost stories he kept archived in his mind. 'I'm afraid not, or rather, thankfully not, since you're sleeping there. No, I really can't say I've ever heard any stories about that part of town.'

'Thanks,' Louise said.

She walked around the information centre for a while and browsed the tacky souvenirs for sale. There were glow-in-the-dark skeletons and plastic spiders, tea towels with images of miners hard at work, as well as postcards and key rings. The only thing she stopped to admire wasn't even for sale. It was a grand old cash register that had been used back in the days when the information centre was a general store. She almost wished it was still being used, because there was no butcher, baker, or grocer in town. Any shopping would have to be done back at Rawson.

'Do you want to buy something?' Oscar asked her.

'No, not here, but I wouldn't mind seeing what goodies they have at the lolly shop next door.'

They stepped outside and walked a few paces down the road to the Old Lolly Shoppe. A small four-wheel drive cruised past at the same time, and its driver, an elegant blonde woman, gave them a friendly lift of the hand from the steering wheel.

"Star Hotel" was written along the side of the vehicle.

The moment they stepped inside the lolly shop was the second creepiest encounter Oscar had yet experienced in Walhalla. The shop itself was quite pretty and took him straight back to his childhood. Shelves were stocked with hundreds of kinds of confectionary, many of which he hadn't seen in years. Redskins, wagon wheels, and warheads were all over the place. There was red and black liquorice tape, rocky road, caramel fudge, coconut ice, as well as chocolate-coated almonds and macadamia nuts. The shop had it all. The creepy part of it was behind the counter, and in the air all around them.

'Hello,' Clarissa's strict face muttered, without an ounce of happiness in its voice. She was a middle-aged woman with short hair that had been dyed black and a horrible pair of glasses that made her look like a school headmistress. The way she stared at Oscar and Louise and the fact that she was listening to hardcore techno made their skin crawl. The music throbbed and the frozen gaze followed them as they walked around the shop, barely daring to speak to each other.

Oscar turned towards her a couple of times to find her staring straight at him. She didn't seem to realise the effect she was having. Did she think they were shoplifters? He wanted to ask her about ghosts, just like he asked everybody, but something told him not to. Was he worried she might actually be one?

'I'm going outside for some fresh air,' he whispered to Louise.

'*Tu ne me laisses pas toute seule avec elle!*' she replied.

She gripped his hand dramatically and pulled him outside.

'Goodbye,' Louise said as naturally as possible.

Clarissa just hummed at them.

'I'm not going back in there,' Oscar told her once they were out of earshot.

'Me neither. I shouldn't eat that sugary rubbish anyway. Who do you want to talk to now?'

'I don't know. We haven't had much luck, have we? I want to forget about this ghost business for a while, as hard as it may be. Let's go back to the tent and get lunch ready.'

Louise agreed. They walked back along the main street and tried to put Oscar's experience out of mind for a while. But both of them knew that once the sun had gone down, Oscar would head straight back to where he'd heard the sobbing. Louise had already decided she'd be going with him.

#

By the time they'd finished a simple lunch of avocado and tinned tuna on rice crackers, more campers had arrived in Walhalla.

A van pulled into the car park and a group of young men scrambled out, yawning and stretching. One of them rushed to the toilets.

'German,' Oscar said.

'Or Swedish.'

The one who'd been driving called out to his friend rushing to the toilets.

'Dutch,' Oscar and Louise said simultaneously.

'Well, there you go. We have some company,' he reassured her.

She smiled. It might have been silly but it did make her feel more comfortable.

When they came back from a walk through the hills to the east of Walhalla, just before nightfall, a family had arrived and pitched their tent not far from Oscar and Louise's. The camping area was becoming a hive of activity. Fires were being lit and children were playing games, but despite it all, Oscar kept thinking about the ghostly sobbing.

8.

Oscar felt safer with Louise by his side as they grabbed their torches and ventured quietly past the tents and vans of their fellow campers. He'd faced some dangerous men in the course of his work, but he'd never been confronted with anything of the supernatural order.

As they approached the spot, he waited for a reaction from Louise.

'I can hear it!' she whispered straight into his ear.

He breathed a sigh of relief. He wasn't crazy after all. But what did it mean?

'Where do you think it's coming from?' he asked her.

Her shoulders shrugged in the torch light. It seemed to be all around.

'I'm a bit scared, Oscar.'

'That's understandable. But I need to know.'

She listened carefully and then pointed up to their right, towards the top of the rock face.

'Up there?'

She nodded apologetically. They both knew what had to be done.

'Hold the torch on the surface in front of me if you can.'

'No problem.'

It was more difficult in the dark, but Oscar succeeded in climbing back up to the rocky ledge, just as he had earlier that day. He pulled a small torch from his pocket and looked around. He could hear the sobbing more clearly.

He shivered as he stepped towards the crack in the embankment and raised his torch, but then, without warning, a vague form rushed at him. He didn't notice where it had come from, maybe out of the rock itself.

He stumbled back towards the track, dropping his torch. He didn't know how he was going to climb back down, but he tried, and even though he descended half of the slope safely, he slipped past the last tree and fell heavily to the ground.

The next thing he knew, Louise was leaning over him, making sure he was all right. Then she looked up towards the rocky ledge and let out a terrifying scream, but by the time Oscar could follow her gaze, the apparition had gone.

They hurried back to the campsite, not daring to utter a word, and Oscar zipped the tent closed behind them with all the precision of a fashion designer testing his latest creation. Louise had never seen him like that before. He was rattled and confused, but not confused the way he had been up until that frightening encounter. It was as though one sense of confusion had vanished and been replaced by another.

'You saw it better than I did,' she started. 'You reacted as though it were a ghost.' She paused and shone the light so that it lit up his face a little. 'It wasn't a ghost, was it?'

'I don't believe in ghosts. You know that, honey,' he said with a nervous wink. His confidence was back, but not entirely.

'A hoax then,' she whispered, looking fearfully at the sides of the tent.

'Somebody pretending to be a ghost,' he mused. 'I don't know what I saw. I mean, it all happened so fast. It didn't look like a ghost though, whatever one is supposed to look like. It wasn't transparent or luminous. It seemed more like somebody wearing a white sheet, effective in the dark and with the element of surprise but ridiculous after more than a quick glance. I think somebody was trying to spook us!'

'And succeeded!' Louise added. 'But why? To attract more tourists? Somebody was sitting on the cliff in the middle of the night dressed up like a ghost and sobbing to him or herself on the off chance a camper would walk by?'

'It doesn't make sense, does it?'

Louise simply shook her head.

'I'm going back there again tomorrow,' Oscar told her. 'I don't care if I'm bruised and scratched. I'm going back there again in broad daylight to have a *really* close look.'

Louise smiled a little. She knew that only a real ghost could escape her husband once he got to work. She rolled over and asked him to hold her until she fell asleep.

9.

In the morning, while Louise and all the campers were still asleep, and the sun and birds were only just beginning to emerge from their slumber, Oscar got ready for his fourth trek up to the spot that had caused him more confusion and self-analysis than any other he had stumbled across in his career. He was determined to get to the bottom of the mystery once and for all.

He ignored the tightness in his muscles as he pulled himself up the breach in the rock face. Strangely enough, it felt less difficult than it had the first two times. He supposed he was getting used to it.

Once at the top, he knelt down and studied the ground where he'd hastened back from the menacing shape that had confronted him, but even though some rain had fallen during the night, the ground was hard and revealed nothing. He stepped through the crack in the embankment and walked towards the bushes growing near the rock face. To his right, the land fell downwards in a gentle slope that curved back to the west. Further along, it flattened out before rising again towards the peak of the mountain. He could see the walking track down below him and realised with annoyance that there was a far easier way of getting to the ledge. He could have simply walked up there, weaving through a few trees and bushes. At least he wouldn't have to climb down the steep breach again.

He frowned. Despite the maze-like nature of the area he found himself in, it didn't seem to be very special, and he couldn't detect any signs of activity.

He sat on the ground and closed his eyes for a moment.

When he opened them again, he observed his surroundings with a fresh perspective. The maze-like nature of the area? But that was just it, wasn't it? It wasn't natural at all.

He jumped up and took a closer look at the rock face around him and the crack in the embankment through which he had come. There were long grooves scarring the surface here and there, as though some giant beast had scratched at the rock with unimaginably hard claws. He'd seen similar marks before at historic sites around the world and recognised them immediately. It was where dynamite had been rammed into holes using metal rods in order to blow a hill apart.

He bent over and scratched maniacally at the ground with his bare hands. The three slick scars on his right hand shone.

Under the still muddy soil was a kind of grey slate, as though he were actually standing on a pile of rubble.

He scurried around in circles like a hound that had caught a whiff of the fox. Some of the ground was hard rock, other parts were damp soil, and then he saw what he'd been hoping to see; faint impressions in the soil, traces of where shoes had been. Lots of them. The remote location had experienced a great deal of traffic in recent times. They weren't very clear, but he could tell where they led. They went straight into bushes growing against a section of rock face.

Oscar bit his lower lip and started to feel better about himself. He'd been crazy to question his sanity. He followed the footprints, and looking all around to make sure that nobody was watching, pushed through the bushes as though intending to walk straight into the rock face.

He found what he'd expected; a rusty gate almost the height of a man with a chain wrapped around it and fastened to the rock itself. There was a faded sign attached to the gate, but no words could be made out. He guessed it had once read *Danger! No Entry!* or something along those lines, but this gate must have been hidden for years. It wasn't obvious like the similar mine entrances he'd noticed closer to the township.

Hidden, but not to everybody.

He looked at the ground. The footprints went into the mine, and one of them wasn't too blurry after all. He pulled his camera out of his backpack and knelt down to take a photo of it. It was the inside tip of a left hiking boot, and the print was clear enough to identify the sole of the boot that had made it. Oscar didn't know why he was gathering clues. He wasn't sure whether giving curious tourists the creeps was a crime punishable by law, but something weird was happening, and his instincts told him to get to the bottom of it. He took a photo of the mine gate too, just for good measure. Then the lock caught his attention. It was a Yale, and, unlike the rusted gate and chain, it was new. He took a photo of it and then, lifting it, took a photo of the keyhole.

'Footprints and locks,' he said, smiling to himself. 'Not the stuff of ghosts.'

He tried the gate, even though he could tell it wouldn't open. All it did was groan crankily. So he took his torch from his backpack and shone it along the mineshaft, but the passage was bare and its darkness swallowed his torch's feeble beam. He put the torch away and took his notebook and pen:

Questions:

a) Who was crying and why was he or she in a mineshaft?

b) Why has the old lock been replaced with a new one? Implies that whoever did it didn't have a key for the original lock, if indeed there was one. Was the lock put there to keep people out or to keep somebody in? Possible link to the first question.

c) Assuming the aim was to keep somebody locked inside and my curiosity resulted in this person being moved to another location, where is the prisoner now?

d) What steps can I take to answer the first three questions?
1. Gather gossip / anybody gone missing / any tension in town? (Louise can help with that)
2. Find the hiking boot that matches the print fragment (difficult)
3. Find the key that unlocks the padlock (very difficult)

Oscar put the notebook away. He knew he would have more questions later, but for the time being, they were enough to get him started.

He was good at picking locks, and a Yale padlock was no challenge at all, but he didn't have the necessary tools with him. He'd left them in the safe hidden under his house in Brisbane. What's more, he wasn't sure whether he wanted to enter the abandoned mine. He suspected the solution to the puzzle was to be found elsewhere. He just wasn't quite sure where to start.

One thing was for sure, he wasn't going to do any more investigating until after breakfast, and he didn't want to press his luck with Louise by disappearing on her for a second time in as many days.

He took the easy way down to the walking track and headed back to the camping area.

#

The Dutch boys were awake and sipping what Oscar could tell by the aroma floating through the crisp air was a deliciously strong brew of coffee. He decided to do likewise. The family camped next to them was also up and about. Mum was frying eggs and baked beans for breakfast while the kids climbed over the picnic table.

'Good morning,' he said as he walked towards his tent.

'Hello. You've been for an early walk, have you?'

'Yes, just stretching the legs,' Oscar replied vaguely. 'Did you sleep well?'

'We did. It's so peaceful here.'

'My name's Oscar.'

'I'm Jane. This is Daniel, Kelly, and Natalie.' She indicted her children in order from eldest to youngest. 'My husband's still asleep.'

'So is my wife.'

'I'm getting up,' Louise called from inside the tent. A moment later, the zipper ripped through the morning air and she emerged, blinking.

'Good morning. I'm Jane. I hope you've slept well.'

'Yes, thank you. My name's Louise.'

'Is this your first time in Walhalla?'

'Yes,' Oscar said. 'And you?'

'No, we've been coming here every year since we got married,' Jane explained, stirring the baked beans. 'We suspect Daniel was conceived here eleven years old.'

Daniel smiled shyly.

'Maybe the same will happen to you,' Jane said, and then smiled awkwardly, hoping her remark would be well received.

'Maybe,' Louise said. 'But it'd probably help if my husband stayed in the tent with me instead of running off into the forest every night.'

Jane laughed.

'You're quite the hiker, I take it?'

Oscar chose his words carefully. 'I just like fresh air and birdsong.'

'I can understand that. What are you up to today?'

'We're doing the ghost tour tonight but we haven't yet discussed our plans for the day. We'll do that now over a coffee,' Louise said.

'You'll absolutely love the ghost tour. We've done it a number of times ourselves, and it's never exactly the same. Anyway, I'm sure we'll see each other around town. Don't let me stop you from getting your breakfast ready.'

'Talk to you later, Jane,' Oscar said before heading off to the toilets. Louise joined him.

'Do you want to boil up some water and have an instant coffee here or drink a cappuccino with our old friend, Fay?'

she asked.

'She's our old friend now, is she? Despite the fact that she wants to steal me from you.'

'Don't flatter yourself! The reason is I can tell you discovered something up at the scene of the haunting this morning and it has nothing to do with ghosts, so I figure you want to get some more information from the locals about what's happening in town.'

Louise walked away from Oscar and disappeared into the ladies' toilets, grinning smugly.

Oscar headed towards the gents', shaking his head and speechless.

10.

The Greyhorse was busy again that morning, but the customers weren't the same as the day before. At the table where the workers had been sitting was a couple in their late sixties or early seventies. The man was reading a newspaper and his wife was staring at her coffee as if in deep contemplation. The man looked up and nodded disinterestedly at Oscar and Louise, before turning back to his paper.

Another couple, roughly the same age, or perhaps a little older, were sitting at the table where the strange couple in hats and sunglasses had been the day before. Both couples looked quite similar to each other, and for a moment, Oscar wondered whether they might be related. But a closer look at their attractive but weathered faces, and the fact that they weren't paying any attention to each other, made him change his mind.

'Back again! Is it my coffee that keeps bringing you back or something else?' She winked at Oscar.

'Your coffee and your company,' he replied.

Louise felt the urge to elbow him in the ribs. She thought about doing the same to Fay as well.

'Take a seat.'

Oscar went over to the table the furthest from the other customers. Louise went inside and grabbed a glossy magazine from the rack near the counter behind which Fay was making their cappuccinos. She was tempted to take advantage of the opportunity to say a few stern words, to tell her to stop flirting with her husband, but Fay smiled at her softly and Louise felt sorry for her. She was a beautiful woman living in a ghost town where the pickings were rare. Sure, it had been her choice to stay in Walhalla, but all the same, Louise couldn't bring herself to broach the subject. She just took a copy of *Famous* and went back outside.

Oscar was staring at the bandstand, but Louise knew he wasn't simply appreciating the nineteenth-century architecture. On the way down from the camping area, he'd told her what he'd found up there and shown her his photographs, but now that they were in public, they couldn't talk so openly.

Louise tried to look at the shoes of the four people sitting on the terrace.

'No such luck,' Oscar said without taking his gaze from the bandstand.

Fay brought their coffees out and was about to go back inside when Oscar decided to engage her in conversation.

'Are most of your customers locals or visitors?'

She took a seat.

'Both really.' She lowered her voice and looked towards the table where the man was reading his newspaper and the woman was staring at the sky. 'The couple over there, Frank and Keri Crain, are locals. They run the Wild Cherry guesthouse, which is up near the old hospital. Their current guests were here at the same time as you yesterday morning. It's a gorgeous guesthouse. They did it up themselves recently. Frank is quite a handyman. Anyway, they're pretty quiet and keep to themselves, but they sure know how to provide great service for their guests. If you get sick of your tent, you should stay there for a night or two.' She leaned closer conspiratorially. 'Mind you, it'll cost you a pretty penny.'

'What about the couple next to them?' Louise asked.

Fay was only too happy to continue feeding their curiosity.

'They're not locals. They're guests at Windsor House, on their fortieth wedding anniversary,' Fay whispered.

'Do they know it's haunted?' Oscar asked, even though his brief encounter with accepting the existence of the supernatural had come to a definitive end earlier that morning.

'Probably. Ghosts don't scare people away though, do they? They pull them in.'

Oscar had to admit she had a point. But people disguised as ghosts could be pretty bloody scary when they lunged at you in the middle of the night.

'Are there a lot of visitors in Walhalla at the moment?'

'There aren't many guests just now, but that should change by Christmas. The Star Hotel usually has one or two couples or small groups at any given time. This weekend, there are three girls staying there. I think they're all recent divorcees who wanted to leave Melbourne for a few days and go somewhere tranquil and void of eligible young men. Unfortunately for them, they haven't escaped the attention of Ned and Walt, the men who have been doing tree clearing and burning off here for the last month or so.'

'Are they the men who were here when we came yesterday?'

'That's right. They come here for breakfast a couple of

mornings a week. Anyway, what was I saying? Oh yes, the other guests here at the moment are the couple I mentioned staying at the Wild Cherry and this couple here from Windsor House. It's a pretty quiet time in Walhalla, even more so than usual. I noticed you have some company up at the camping area. That's good, isn't it?'

'Yes,' Louise confirmed. 'I feel more comfortable now.'

'So, you're going on the ghost tour tonight?'

'We certainly are,' Oscar confirmed. 'I've got my lamp and camera ready.'

'You'll love it. What are you doing before then?'

'I wanted to walk around town some more,' Oscar said. 'You know, check out some of the old sites.'

Frank and Keri got up from their table and headed off around the café to where their four-wheel drive was parked.

'See you later, Fay,' Frank called out. 'Off to do our shopping.'

'See you.'

Ben appeared from around the bend to the south, and Oscar had to wonder whether the owners of the Wild Cherry had somehow sensed his arrival and hurried off in order to avoid having to convince him they weren't interested in buying whatever he was selling. They needn't have worried, as it turned out, because Ben wasn't carrying any bags at all. He stared at everybody at the café, but particularly at Fay and Louise. He had barely acknowledged their existence the day before in his attempt to secure a deal with Oscar. Now, with nothing to hawk, he stared at them lewdly, as though trying to see the forms of their breasts through their clothes. Then he went along on his merry way.

A woman arrived from the other direction. She had long grey hair and thin features, and despite her smile, her face betrayed underlying sadness.

'Hello, Andrea,' Fay called out.

'Good morning. How's everything today, dear?'

'Not bad at all, and you?'

'Just fine. I might pop in for a coffee later.'

'All right then.'

Fay turned back to Oscar and Louise. 'That's Andrea Collins. She lives at Tainsh Cottage with her husband, Gerald. He grew up in Walhalla. He's one of the few locals who did. They're both retired now but keep themselves busy enough.'

'You get along well with her?' Louise asked.

'Absolutely. She's not exactly a barrel of laughs, especially since she lost her son, but she's a remarkable woman.'

'Her son went missing?' Oscar knew it was a long shot.

Fay frowned. 'Missing? No. He was killed in an accident.'

'I see,' Oscar hastened to say. 'That's terrible. What about the woman at the lolly shop?'

'Clarissa. What about her?'

'Are you friends with her?'

Fay looked around nervously, as though worried that the subject of their conversation might be within earshot, but Oscar guessed she was behind the counter of her shop, listening to techno.

'She's a weird one. I don't think anybody in town talks to hear. Luckily for us, she just works here. She lives in Rawson.'

'Are there any other strange sorts like her around?'

'I think we're all fairly strange here, don't you? Well, who else is there? There's Les at the information centre. You've met him, I suppose. He's pretty boring really, but he knows a lot about the town. He's not married and probably never will be. He only believes in small talk or chatting about the lives of people long dead. I don't know much about him. There are the owners of Windsor House. Did I mention them? Karl and Chelsea Gloz. I'm very good friends with them. We often have dinner together.'

'Well,' Oscar said with a tone of finality. 'We'd better be off. We've taken up enough of your time already.'

Fay glanced around. All her customers had left.

'Suit yourselves. I'll see you around town. Enjoy your ghost tour tonight.'

They thanked her and headed off down the street.

'She's a treasure trove when it comes to getting information on the locals,' Louise said.

'She is indeed, but gossips aren't always accurate.'

'She didn't mention that anybody had gone missing.'

'No,' Oscar replied. He stroked his moustache and stared at the ground.

'What does that mean?'

'It could mean one of several things. It could mean that she's hiding something, or that some topics are so taboo even a gossip like her won't broach them with strangers, or that she's unaware somebody has gone missing.'

Louise nodded.

'But I think that one explanation is more likely than any of those,' he continued.

'What's that?'

'What do you think?'

Louise didn't know what other explanation there could be, except that Oscar was wrong.

'That you're on the wrong track,' she said.

He frowned. 'Well, that's another possibility again, but I was thinking that nobody from town has gone missing after all.'

It was Louise's turn to frown. 'Isn't that the same thing?'

'No, of course not. It's completely different. I need to go for a long walk by myself. Do you mind?'

Louise shrugged. She knew her husband's ways. 'Fine, I'll keep myself busy. Meet me back at the tent for lunch at one o'clock.'

He saluted her and jogged off towards the long flight of stairs leading up to the Tramline Walkway.

11.

Louise found herself in the art and craft shop, just down the road from the lolly shop. There was no market in town, but she was relieved to have stumbled across at least one shop of interest, and she ended up meeting a woman who was quite possibly the only person in town to have escaped Fay's gossip. She wore an enchanting bohemian dress and had auburn hair without a hint of grey.

Her shop was a gallery showcasing everything from photographs, portraits, and landscape paintings to patchwork quilts, wooden toys, and carved statuettes. There was also an impressive array of handmade jewellery, but Louise resisted the temptation.

'Good morning.'

'Good morning. This is a beautiful shop,' Louise said.

'Thank you. Most of my stock is local. We have quite a few talented artists in Walhalla.'

'Were the panoramic shots taken by a local?'

'They weren't. They were taken by a professional photographer who paid himself a helicopter flight along the valley. Spectacular, aren't they?'

'Absolutely,' Louise agreed. 'And the paintings?'

'We have a couple of painters in town. The landscapes were

done by Karl Gloz, he has such a great name for a painter, don't you think? Karl manages Windsor House, one of the guesthouses.'

'Yes, Fay up at The Greyhorse told me about him.'

She rolled her eyes and tutted. 'Fay tells everybody about everybody else. She can't be trusted with a secret, that girl. What did she tell you about me?'

'Nothing, as a matter of fact. You must be one of the only locals she didn't mention at all.'

'I suppose I'm just not interesting enough to make an appearance in her gossip.' She extended her hand. 'My name is Deirdre, and my husband, who works out of town, is Archie. Neither of us have had an affair, or worship the devil, or keep any other skeletons in our closets. That's probably why you haven't heard about us.'

'I'm Louise. My husband and I are camping in town for a while.'

'That's wonderful. You're from France, right?'

'Yes, I am. My husband is from Brisbane.'

'Well, I hope you have a good time in Walhalla. If you do decide to buy anything bulky, I can arrange a special rate for postage.'

'I'll keep that in mind,' Louise answered.

She took a closer look at the portraits and immediately recognised the subjects of two of them. One of them was of Ben Fordyce and an older woman who could only have been his mother, Helen. It seemed such a strangely personal portrait to have on display in a public place, although Louise wasn't quite sure why she felt that way. The other was of Clarissa from the Old Lolly Shoppe. The artist had captured her fake smile perfectly. Her face was pale and her regard almost menacing. It formed a chilling contrast with the bright colours of lollies that hung temptingly on the wall behind her.

A little further along the wall was a portrait of a young man with a face that was both gentle and strong. He was standing next to a grilled gate that seemed to be the entrance to the Extended Long Tunnel Mine. Louise didn't recognise him.

'Those remarkable portraits are the work of Keri Crain. Keri and Frank own the Wild Cherry guesthouse. I'm not sure why, but guesthouses and art seem to go hand in hand in Walhalla.'

'They certainly do. Are the managers of the Star Hotel artists too?'

'Michael and Stephanie? My word, no. I guess you could say business is their art.'

Deirdre swept her arm to the left and indicated a whole aisle of other handicrafts. 'The wooden statuettes and carvings are the work of Gerald Collins. He lives at Tainsh Cottage with his wife Andrea. Stunning, aren't they? And those patchwork quilts were made by Helen Fordyce who lives in Spetts Cottage.'

'Very impressive,' Louise said. 'I had no idea there was so much talent here.'

'There's something about Walhalla that attracts creative people.'

'Do you have any jokers in town—people who like to have a laugh at the expense of others?'

Deirdre was obviously surprised by the question. She thought for a moment. 'I really don't think anybody in town has enough of a sense of humour to play tricks, and even though some of the locals can be a bit strange, nobody's outright nasty.'

Louise knew Oscar wouldn't have approved, but she'd decided Deirdre seemed like an honest woman.

'My husband thinks somebody is playing a joke on him,

dressing up like a ghost and crying in the middle of the night.'

Deirdre was horrified. 'Who would do such a thing? Was this at the camping area?'

'Close, on the walking track.'

'It must be one of the other campers. None of the locals would do that.'

'I suppose, only there weren't any other campers there when it happened.'

Deirdre opened her mouth to speak, but then thought better of it.

'What is it?' Louise encouraged her.

'Nothing.'

'You think there's another explanation, don't you? I'm listening.'

'Are you an open-minded person?'

'Do I believe in ghosts? I think I do. I mean, I'm not sure. But this definitely wasn't a ghost.'

Deirdre looked apologetic, as though any incorrect behaviour carried out on a visitor by a local was an affront to her own conscience. 'I don't know what to say, dear. I'll let you know if I hear about anybody playing jokes like that. It certainly comes as a surprise to me.'

'Don't worry. It's probably nothing.'

Louise walked down the aisle where the wooden statuettes and patchwork quilts were, asking herself whether she'd made a big mistake.

12.

Oscar was heading to the abandoned mine entrance again. He wasn't quite sure why he wanted to go back, but Fay's gossip hadn't cleared the mystery up one little bit, so he figured it was the only hope he had of working out what had happened. He needed something to go on, a fragment of a boot print and a photograph of a padlock keyhole may have been enough to assure him that he hadn't been spooked by a phantom, but they weren't solid enough clues to help him make sense of what had happened. He still needed to answer his number one question; who had he heard sobbing and where was that person now? He regretted that he'd been too hasty in brushing off the scene of the strange encounter. Perhaps there were more clues beyond the chained gate. The main problem was whether he could pick the lock without his tools.

He walked up the easy path and parted the bushes again so he could see the gate. He was still thinking about how he could pick the lock when he discovered that the padlock and the chain were no longer there.

They'd simply disappeared.

It had obviously happened in the last few hours. He wondered who could have done it, but that was impossible to answer. Anybody could have gone up there while he'd been eating breakfast at the campsite, chatting with Fay at the café, or walking down the street with Louise or along the track by himself. It only took a few seconds to slip a key into a lock and remove a chain. No, the question of who was one that he couldn't even consider answering with any certainty.

'Why?' he whispered aloud. 'To lock something away in a new safe, or somebody away in a new prison. Where?'

He grabbed the rusted old gate and pulled. It moved noisily but easily outwards. He was able to just walk on in. So, taking his torch from his backpack, he ventured into the unwelcoming darkness of the abandoned mineshaft.

The long corridor pierced deep into the mountainside with only a subtle downward slope. The wooden frames that supported the shaft were still in place but didn't look very reassuring.

Making his way slowly, he swept the torchlight across the ground, not only to make sure he didn't trip on the half-buried sections of rail that hadn't been removed from the shaft, but also so he didn't miss any clues. He was hoping to find an indication that someone had been in there recently.

Every few metres, he turned around and looked at the entrance. The rectangle of daylight filtered through leaves was getting smaller all the time. The light from his torch became weaker as the darkness thickened around him.

Oscar wasn't worried about the tunnel collapsing on him, and he certainly wasn't frightened of ghosts. The disturbing thought that kept nagging at him was that somebody had seen him step into the shaft and would push the gate closed, wrap the chain around it, and click the padlock into place. He imagined himself trapped in there, destined to do the sobbing that had drawn him there in the first place.

At any rate, there was no need to venture further. There was no sign that anybody or anything other than dust and rocks had ever been in the mine at all. Like the gold that it had been dug to find, whatever else it had held was gone without a trace. The only footprints in the tunnel were his own.

Oscar turned and walked back towards the light. The return journey was much faster. He pushed the gate closed behind him and stepped over the prints on the now dry ground at the entrance. He had to find the owner of those tell-tale boots.

Back at the tent, Louise was whipping up a dip using avocado and cream cheese. The other campers were away, perhaps hiking in the mountains or strolling through town.

Oscar realised she was upset about something.

'What's wrong?'

'It's the earrings I bought at the market in Melbourne.'
'Don't tell me you've lost them already.'
She shook her head emphatically. 'They've been stolen!'
'Are you absolutely sure? You've probably just misplaced them. You know how forgetful you are.'
'No, no, no! They've been stolen.'
'Where did you leave them?'
'In the little pocket attached to the insect mesh. Who would go into another person's tent and steal a woman's earrings?'
'A thief would,' Oscar replied. 'So, now I have two mysteries to solve.'
'It seems so,' she said. 'Here, have a glass of wine and relax for a while. You can get back to work later. I want you to find out who took them, even if we have to change our flight back to Brisbane.'
'Are you serious?'
She glowered at him. 'It's a matter of principle!'
Oscar sipped his wine. He now had two mysteries to solve, and although he had no idea which was the more serious of the two, or the more solvable, he had to do whatever he could. But first, lunch, a few more glasses of wine, and a lot of thinking.

Oscar's thinking time turned into emptying the bottle of wine and falling asleep in the tent. When he woke, it was almost dark. Louise was asleep beside him, and the voices in English and Dutch beyond the tent's thin walls informed him that the other campers had returned. He hadn't spoken to the Dutch boys, but he didn't figure them as thieves, and the couple camped beside them seemed so nice it was beyond belief to even suspect them of such a petty act of opportunism.

He yawned and suddenly remembered they had a ghost tour to do that night. Mysteries to solve or not, he wasn't going to miss that.

'Louise,' he whispered. 'Louise.'

'Yes,' she groaned, waking up. 'Have you found my earrings yet?'

'Don't worry. You'll get them back,' he said, trying to sound confident. 'We have the ghost tour tonight. Remember?'

'Oh yeah, so we do. I might just stay here instead.'

'No, you can't. Please, come with me,' he pleaded.

'I'm sad.'

'Because of your earrings?'

'Yes. I liked them so much.'

'What if one of the women at the ghost tour is wearing them?'

'You think that's possible?'

'I don't think it's probable, but I wouldn't rule out the possibility if I were you.'

'All right. Are you hungry?'

'No, maybe after the ghost tour if it's not too late.'

'I'd like to take a shower.'

'So would I, but we can't. You know that.'

Louise frowned. 'We can tomorrow, at the public pool in Rawson.'

'That'd be nice. We could go for a swim at the same time.'

'Have you got the tickets?'

'Yes. Do I smell of wine?'

Louise nodded. 'Big time.'

'Oh well, too bad. I'm going outside to stretch my legs and get some fresh air. Join me when you're ready.'

He unzipped the insect mesh and crawled out of the tent. The sun was setting and the air was growing cold again. Haunting time, he thought to himself. He wished the haunting would reoccur. If he heard the sobbing again, he wouldn't miss the chance to find its source.

13.

Anne Saunders looked just like she had in the portrait. Her long scarlet and black dress glowed under the lamplight outside the Walhalla Print Shop, where the ghost tour was set to start.

The three Dutch boys were there. They had arrived just before Oscar and Louise and were smoking and chatting together while they subtly checked out the young divorcees, Emily, Deana, and Wendy. The girls had obviously been drinking and were giggling loudly and making spooky noises to scare each other. Wendy crept up behind Emily and pinched her bottom. Emily let out a high-pitched scream and the Dutch boys smiled approvingly.

'It wasn't me! It was the ghost of Jeremy!' Wendy pleaded.

'Jeremy isn't a ghost. He doesn't even have a soul! And he's not dead!'

'Unfortunately!' Deana yelled.

All three of them roared with laughter.

Anne tried not to smile. It would have ruined her grave persona.

'Good evening, ladies and gentlemen, on this most terrifying of evenings,' the guide welcomed them. 'The tour will begin shortly. We're just waiting on a few more people.'

Louise stared at the divorcees' ears, and one of them, noticing that she was being examined intensely, replied silently with a defiant glare.

'Stop that, please,' Oscar whispered. 'None of them are wearing your earrings.'

'That doesn't mean they didn't steal them,' she whispered back.

'No, it doesn't, but I don't want to have to break up a

catfight.'

The couple staying at the Wild Cherry appeared out of the darkness, causing Deana to scream with fright.

'They're not ghosts, you idiot!' Emily scolded her.

'Sorry,' she said. But the couple didn't say anything. They just ignored the young women.

'They're not very sociable those two, are they?' Louise whispered.

Oscar didn't reply. He just watched the newcomers with curiosity.

'Good evening, Mr and Mrs Munnings,' Anne said. 'We have two more joining us. I think they'll be here shortly.'

One of the Dutch boys put his cigarette out and edged slowly towards Deana as though he wanted to engage her in conversation, but she just frowned at him and he stopped in his tracks.

Oscar guessed that the retired couple staying at Windsor House would be the final two to join the group, since, as far as he was aware, they were the only other visitors in town who hadn't already been on the tour.

A moment later, the couple arrived and greeted the assembly. 'Good evening. My name is Peter, and this is my wife, Faith. Our apologies for being a little tardy, but the spread at Windsor House is simply fantastic.'

His polite words were warmly received, and Anne Saunders agreed on his assessment of the Windsor House dining experience.

Wendy made a remark about her ex-husband's appreciation of a good spread being a major part of the problem with him, but the joke seemed to go right over the retired couple's heads. It was likewise lost on the Dutch boys, much to the amusement of Deana and Emily.

'Good evening, ladies and gentlemen. My name is Anne Saunders. I'm going to take you on a dark and haunting tour of Walhalla. The quaint township in which you find yourselves today is quiet and pretty, but let me assure you, this was once one of the busiest gold mining towns in Victoria. Thousands rushed here to seek their fortunes, but many met a terrible end. Poverty, disease, and violence were rife in the Walhalla of the nineteenth century.'

The group was speechless.

'I don't know whether you believe in ghosts, but I can tell you that I absolutely do. I can't guarantee that you will feel the presence of the departed as we walk through the town tonight, but people often do on this tour. All I can say is that you ought to keep your wits about you and your minds open. Take photos if you like. Sometimes cameras detect what we cannot. However, spirits don't always want to be photographed, and you may find that your camera refuses to work in some troubled parts of the town.'

The group gasped, and those who had cameras, which was everybody except for Peter and Faith, checked that they were functioning.

'Could I ask you your names and where you come from before we embark on our journey of dark discovery?'

She turned towards the Dutch boys.

'My name is Dirk, and this is Henk and Ignaas. We're from the Netherlands.'

'I'm Oscar, and this is Louise. I'm from Brisbane, and Louise is from France.'

'Nice to meet you,' Anne said, then turned to the women.

'I'm Wendy, and my friends are Deana and Emily. We're from Melbourne. We're all recently divorced, so we decided to come up here to clear our heads a little.'

'Well, Walhalla is a great place to clear your heads. There are some men here, but most of them are already spoken for and shouldn't bother you. There are a couple you might want to watch out for though.' Anne winked at them.

'Yeah, we've met Ned and Walt. I think they got the message.'

Everybody laughed.

'Good to hear,' Anne said. 'What about you?'

'My name is Harvey, and this is my wife, Christina. We're from Melbourne,' the man informed everybody.

'Now, you haven't been married for forty years, have you?'

'No, not that long just yet,' Harvey answered.

Christina laughed nervously and scratched an eyebrow.

Oscar and Louise exchanged a glance.

'*We* are celebrating our fortieth anniversary,' corrected Faith. 'Peter and I.'

A round of applause exploded, and the young divorcees shook their heads in admiration bordering on disbelief.

'Tonight, you're going to hear a few loves stories, but, alas, they are tragic tales of loves lost and promises unfulfilled.'

'That sounds familiar,' Wendy mumbled loud enough for all to hear. The others didn't know whether to laugh.

'I'll start by giving you a lantern each. If you have your own torches, feel free to use them as well,' Anne explained as she started handing out electric lanterns that looked vaguely similar to their oil-fuelled ancestors. 'We're going to walk down to Windsor House, where Peter and Faith are staying. However, I should warn them that after this tour, they might be tempted to seek refuge on more hallowed ground.'

The group gasped.

The retired couple smiled to hide their nervousness.

Anne walked down to the main street, her lantern swinging

at her side and casting a pale light that danced flippantly across the bitumen. She walked elegantly past the site of the old pub and turned right, leading the group along the narrow street behind The Greyhorse and Star Hotel. That street followed the course of one branch of Stringers Creek. Its most notable edifice was Windsor House, the two-storey home that had been built by the Gloz family so many years ago and continued to be held and preserved by Karl Gloz.

Anne stopped outside the stately brick home.

The sound of flowing water, the gentle glow of the moon, and the lamplight made for a romantic setting, but Anne knew the ghastly secrets of that building. On the other side of the short footbridge crossing the creek, a white picket gate with a brass plaque was closed. The building itself was in darkness, except for a lamp hanging at the front door and light shining through the curtains of the upstairs window on the far left.

'Our light's on,' Peter said aloud. 'Didn't we turn it off?'

'Yes. I turned it off before we left,' Faith stated with certainty.

'You're sleeping in *that* room?' Anne asked.

'We are. Why?' Faith asked reluctantly.

'Did you sleep well last night?'

'Very well, as a matter of fact,' Peter said.

'Strange stories have been told about that room,' Anne informed them. 'People have reported waking up in the middle of the night to find a young girl standing at the foot of their bed or walking through the walls. Some of our colleagues from Beechworth, a man and a woman, came and stayed there one night, but the key wouldn't work. They couldn't open the door. What happened next sends a chill down my spine every time I recount it.'

The group was silent and the tension was heavy in the air.

'The woman's mobile phone rang, and when she answered it, all she could hear was a little girl calling, 'Mummy! Mummy!' But the girl wouldn't say anything else. Then, all of a sudden, the key worked and the door swung open.'

Anne observed the group closely.

'Have any of you tried making a call from Walhalla?'

'I can't get reception,' Dirk complained.

Anne nodded ominously. 'Nobody can. There is no mobile reception on the valley floor of Walhalla.'

They gasped.

'Karl didn't warn you?' Anne asked Peter and Faith.

'Not in such specific terms,' Peter replied.

Anne just smiled and shrugged her puffy scarlet shoulders.

'Let's move on, shall we?' she announced cheerily.

The group continued to Spetts Cottage, where Anne told the story of Rhoda in her wedding dress. They then headed up to the old school building and continued on to the Extended Long Tunnel Mine, where miners' ghosts still haunted the shafts and a schoolgirl had been decapitated by a mine trolley.

After that, the procession headed south again along the Tramline Walkway and stopped at the lookout. Anne shone her spotlight across the valley and onto the mountainside opposite, where a magnificent old building with gabled roofs and a long verandah appeared to be suspended in the darkness like a chandelier in a dimensionless ballroom.

'The old hospital, which has been closed to the public and under renovation for many years. Have you heard about Emily?' She turned to the divorcee who carried the same name. 'Not you of course, my dear.'

Silence.

'Emily was a nurse whose beloved worked in the mines until he fell gravely ill and was sent to hospital. We're not sure what disease struck him, but there were plenty to choose from in gold rush towns in those days. She tended to him as best she could, for she was madly in love with him and they intended to marry. Unfortunately, all her attention and tenderness was to no avail. He passed away, and she, heartbroken, hanged herself.'

'That's dreadful,' Louise said softly.

'The poor child,' Faith added.

'A tragic love story,' Anne mused. 'The old hospital used to be a guesthouse, and hopefully will be again one day. Guests used to sleep in the old hospital beds.'

'Are you serious?' Deana asked. 'That's so morbid.'

'Not everybody's cup of tea when it comes to a weekend getaway, but we seem to attract somewhat peculiar visitors here.' She paused just long enough to offer them a cheeky grin. 'Emily's presence has been felt in the old building. Some mentioned the door at one end of the former ward being opened and closed, and then the door at the other end being opened and closed a few seconds later, as though a nurse doing her rounds had passed through.'

Anne took the light off the old hospital and, as it swung in an arc across the ground, noticed an object at her feet. She bent over and picked it up.

'A school cap,' she announced, examining the item of headwear. She held it up for the group to see. 'Does this belong to anybody here? No, none of you have school age children, do you? Maybe you, Mr and Mrs Munnings?'

They shook their heads.

Oscar held his lamp up towards the cap, but his gesture was merely a decoy. He was actually observing the faces and movements of the other members of the group with practised subtlety.

Nobody seemed to be interested at all. They just wanted to hear a few more spooky stories before heading back to their tents or bedrooms for wine, sleep, or sex. At the beginning of the tour, the Dutch boys had been hoping for a taste of the latter, but as the night dragged on, they lost all hope of winning the attention of the three divorcees.

'Scotch College,' Anne said, reading the stitching on the cap. 'Isn't that one of the most prestigious schools in Melbourne?'

There were several hums of agreement.

Wendy's reaction was less ambivalent. 'That's where my ex-husband went to school. For all the money his filthy rich parents spent on his education, you would have thought they could at least teach him how to respect women.'

'Keep looking until you find a man who deserves you,' Faith said.

'I have a lighter,' Wendy continued. 'Let's burn it!'

Everybody laughed.

'I'll just take it to lost property in case the owners come asking,' Anne said. She then started back towards the stairs that would lead the group down past the Masonic Lodge and the bandstand. The tour was drawing to a close.

Once the others had returned their lanterns and said goodnight, Oscar asked Louise to wait a moment longer. He had a couple of important questions for Anne.

'Thank you, Anne. That was an intriguing tour. I was just wondering; can you tell me a little about the abandoned mines around Walhalla?'

'Of course. What do you want to know?'

'Are there many mineshafts along the walking track?'

'Yes, quite a few. Many of them have collapsed over the years, and those that haven't are locked up because they're dangerous. They aren't open to the public.'

'I understand that. I don't want to enter them, but I'd like to take some photos of the gates.'

'Very well, but be careful where you walk. There's one old entrance up near the camping area, but it's probably overgrown nowadays.'

Oscar feigned ignorance.

'There are a couple further south, towards the old bakery, but they're quite high up the mountainside. They could very well be covered in earth or vines and bushes. There probably isn't much left to see of them.'

'Thanks all the same.'

'It's a pleasure. Have a good night, and sweet dreams.'

'Good night,' Oscar said as he took Louise by the hand. Then, when they were out of earshot, he told her, 'My sweet dreams are going to have to wait. I need to go for a walk again.'

He was about to run off when Louise grabbed him by the wrist and said, 'Can't you at least walk me back to the tent first? Believe it or not, I don't feel like strolling alone in the dark right now.'

14.

It took Oscar close to three hours of scrambling over rubble and pushing through bushes to find the two entrances on the section of the walking track overlooking the old bakery. He slipped on loose rocks and stumbled into deep pockets where the ground had collapsed into the disused tunnels beneath, but managed to escape with only a blow to his self-esteem.

The two gates he found didn't have chains and padlocks locking them. They'd been welded shut.

He returned to the lookout where Anne had shown the group the old hospital building across the valley. He sat cross-legged in the cold dark, stroking his moustache pensively as a dozen confused ideas and images floated through his mind like butterflies.

Louise's earrings dangled hypnotically in front of him. A hiking boot trudged past. A chain and Yale padlock snaked across his mind's eye. A van without its headlights on rumbled along, but he hadn't seen it clearly and so only saw a single brake light and heard its engine in his mind. He also heard the sobbing and wished he could hear it once more for real. He saw a boy wearing a Scotch College school cap. The faces of everybody he had met or even merely seen in Walhalla paraded along the corridor of his consciousness. Only, he hadn't yet met or seen everybody in town. Did all these people and objects have a connection to the mystery, or just some of them?

He stood up and leaned against the railing of the lookout. Walhalla was hidden in darkness below. There were no streetlights in the township, but some of its more prominent features, like the bandstand and Star Hotel, were illuminated from below with soft orange lighting.

The headlights of a car appeared from further up the road, somewhere near the camping area, and weaved down through the darkness, disappearing behind buildings or trees here and there like a pair of fireflies in love. Oscar watched as the car continued downhill. He didn't recognise it.

It must have been close to one o'clock in the morning, perhaps even later, but it was apparent that not everybody in town was asleep.

He started walking down the stairs leading between the Masonic Lodge and the bandstand and was about to cross the bridge leading to the road when, right in front of him, the door to the Star Hotel opened quietly and one of the Dutch boys slipped outside.

Oscar hoped he wouldn't be noticed, but he was, and the midnight lover gave him a broad smile and a wink before heading back towards the camping area.

'How the devil did you manage that?' Oscar asked himself under his breath. He'd been so sure that the Dutch boys didn't stand a chance of cracking those hard eggs. He took it as a lesson to be learned. Avoid making assumptions at all costs. That was one of the keys to solving seemingly impossible puzzles.

He wondered which girl he'd been with, or maybe he'd...no, surely not! Again, Oscar reminded himself to avoid assumptions and not let his imagination run *too* wild.

He decided to go for a walk around town.

15.

Louise woke up earlier than Oscar for a change and accepted Jane's invitation to join them for breakfast before they packed up to go home. The Dutch boys were up and drinking coffee. Two of them seemed to be arguing with the other one.

'How was the ghost tour?' Jane asked as she poured Louise a cup of coffee. 'Milk?'

'No, thanks. Oh, it was excellent. I was really quite scared afterwards.'

Jane laughed. 'It *is* scary, isn't it?'

'I want to go on the ghost tour,' her son mumbled between mouthfuls of Weetbix.

'It's for adults only.'

Louise smiled at him. They were good kids, all three of

them. He smiled back at her, and the youngest, Natalie, giggled. But Kelly wasn't in such a good mood and just stared at her bowl of cereal.

'Louise talks funny, doesn't she?' Jane said to Natalie. 'That's because she's from France. Do you know where that is?'

Natalie shook her head.

'A long way from here,' Louise said. 'Too far!'

'Do you get back to see your folks from time to time?'

'I try to go back every eighteen months or so, but it's not always possible.'

Louise looked around. The Dutch boys had stopped arguing and finished their coffee. They were getting ready to leave.

'We're going to be alone again tonight, I suppose.'

'Probably,' Jane said. 'You still haven't decided when you're leaving?'

She didn't want to tell her that she wanted to stay until Oscar found her missing earrings or worked out why he'd heard somebody sobbing along the walking track and been attacked by a pretend ghost, so she just said they'd talk about it during the day.

After breakfast, Jane and the kids helped Mark clean up the campsite, and Louise went for a walk down to The Greyhorse.

'Where's your darling husband?' Fay asked her as soon as she arrived.

'He's still asleep.' *Sorry to disappoint you*, she wanted to add.

'He's a bit of an insomniac, is he?' she asked with a smile that was difficult to interpret.

'When his mind is occupied, he finds it difficult to sleep.'

'His mind certainly seemed occupied last night,' Fay observed.

'You spoke to him?'

'No, I just noticed him walking around from my window. Maybe he was hunting ghosts.'

'Maybe,' Louise agreed. 'He has a vivid imagination.'

'You're a lucky woman, Louise. He's an exceptional man. I can tell.'

'Thank you, but what exactly was he doing near your window?'

Fay laughed. 'I'm pretty sure he wasn't spying on me. He just loitered in the street for a while and then strolled off towards Windsor House.'

'He can be a strange creature sometimes,' Louise said.

'There are plenty of those around here. I can assure you of that. So, just the one cappuccino today?'

'I guess so.'

The distant sound of chainsaws roared into life and echoed across the valley, bringing an end to the peaceful atmosphere.

'That will be Ned and Walt getting on with the job. By the sound of it, they're up near the camping area,' Fay said. 'Perhaps Oscar won't be sleeping much longer.'

'Too bad for him. Are Ned and Walt still trying their luck with the girls staying next door?'

'They tried but soon got the message. The poor fellows, they don't have much luck with the ladies.'

'Do they try their luck with you?'

Fay grinned. 'Ned gave it a shot a while back, just after my ex had left town, but I wasn't interested, and now we're friends, so, you know.'

'I know. They're in the friend zone.'

'Anyway, they're not my style. I'm more into the quiet, dark horse rather than the mountain man.'

Louise understood perfectly.

The Dutch boys drove past in their van and waved to Louise and Fay as they left town.

'I didn't really get a chance to talk to them,' Louise said. 'I suppose they're off on an adventure around the country, maybe to a busier place after the calm of Walhalla.'

Fay made an enigmatic humming sound.

'What is it?'

'I shouldn't say.'

'Don't give me that. You have to tell me.'

'All right, if you insist. Stephanie, from the hotel next door, came down for a coffee earlier this morning and told me she'd been reading last night and was just about to go to sleep when she heard creaking on the stairs.'

'And?'

'She went out of her bedroom to have a look in the corridor and saw a young man leaving the hotel.'

'It was one of the Dutch boys?'

'Well, she couldn't say for sure, but she said he appeared to be in his early twenties. We thought about who it could have been and decided it had to be one of them. So much for their girls-only weekend!'

'Are they staying in separate rooms?'

'I don't know. I suppose so. Oh, I see what you're getting at! What a delicious thought!'

They burst out laughing.

'I'll go and get you a cappuccino. On the house today.'

'Thanks, Fay.'

Harvey and Christina Munnings arrived at the café while Fay was inside and sat down at the same table as last time.

'Good morning,' Louise said. 'You didn't have too many nightmares after the tour?'

'No,' Harvey said. 'We slept like logs. That said, it was a

little more unsettling than I'd expected.'

'I agree. The stories were quite chilling, weren't they? What about the couple at Windsor House with their bedroom light left switched on. She insisted she'd turned it off before leaving.'

'It must be a set-up,' Christina said, coming out of her shell for a change. 'Anne and the Gloz couple must do it as a joke.'

'Anne doesn't play jokes,' Fay called from inside. 'Stranger occurrences than bedroom lights turning themselves on happen at Windsor House all the time.'

Louise and the others just looked at each other in silence.

'At any rate, it was certainly worth the twenty-five dollars,' he said. 'We're leaving today. Back to our real lives.'

Christina bit her bottom lip, and Louise couldn't help but feel suspicious of the timid woman. She wondered what Oscar thought about them both.

'What will you have today?' Fay called out.

'Two large flat whites and a slice of chocolate cake, please,' Harvey replied.

Helen Fordyce came strolling down the street with Gerald and Andrea Collins. Helen was carrying a patchwork quilt and Gerald had a carved statuette of a cockatoo with its crest up and wings out. They were obviously new additions for Deirdre's art and craft shop. Louise thought it was marvellous. She sometimes wished she could leave Brisbane and settle down in a nice community like Walhalla where people supported each other like that.

Helen spotted Louise and whispered to Andrea and Gerald. They turned to look at the young woman coldly, as though she were the cause of some considerable annoyance. But Helen was smiling as she split off from her companions and strode straight over to the café terrace.

'Hello there. Louise, isn't it?'

Louise was taken by surprise.

'Yes,' she replied, not even trying to hide her bewilderment. 'That's right. I can tell by your quilts that you're Helen. They're simply gorgeous. Deirdre spoke to me about you, and I saw a portrait of you and Ben in her shop.'

Helen frowned. 'Oh, I really don't know why I agreed to that. It's horrible. I mean, the portrait is fine, Keri is an amazing artist, but Ben and I weren't at our best that day. Is your husband around?'

'He's still asleep as far as I know. Then again, I never really know with him.'

Helen laughed. 'What an intriguing man he is!'

'So everybody keeps saying.'

'He's quite the detective.'

Louise's jaw dropped.

'He told you that?'

'No, I just mean he's good at solving puzzles,' she replied, raising her eyebrows in surprise.

Louise felt like kicking herself.

'Do you like this quilt?'

'It's beautiful. The orange and burgundy give an immediate impression of warmth.'

Helen held it out to her. 'Please, it's yours.'

'What do you mean?'

'Take it, as a token of my appreciation, and do thank your husband for me again.'

'I don't understand. Thank him for what?'

Helen was dumbstruck. 'He didn't tell you?'

'No, he didn't.'

'Nevertheless, that's none of my business. Please, just thank him for me.'

'I will,' Louise assured her.

Helen smiled warmly and caught up with Gerald and Andrea.

'What games have you been playing, dear husband?' she whispered to herself.

'One cappuccino for you.' Fay placed the mug on the table. 'And two flat whites and a slice of chocolate cake for you.' She looped over to where Harvey and Christina were seated.

A four-wheel drive rolled down the street. Mark was at the wheel, with Jane in the passenger seat and the kids in the back. They all waved at Louise as they went past, except for Kelly, who still seemed to be in a foul mood.

'Goodbye, Louise,' Jane called out. 'Oh, and by the way, Oscar is up. The chainsaws must have got to him. He told me to tell you to stay here and that he'll be down in a few minutes.'

'Thanks. Have a safe trip home!'

Good, she thought to herself, it appeared that he had some explaining to do. She would have to give him a lecture, for the hundredth time, on not keeping his wife in the dark.

16.

When Oscar eventually came strolling around the corner, he had company of the extraordinarily hirsute variety. For a brief instant, Louise thought that it was a woman and started wondering what it was in the rainwater that made them all so gaga about her husband. But it only took a second to realise that the dark brown hair with streaks of grey belonged to a body that was far from feminine. The man was a little taller than Oscar, and, despite wearing a long flowing green cloak that she'd taken to be a dress at first glance, she could tell that he was of a slim but tough build. He wore a long goatee and dark sunglasses and was carrying a handwoven basket full of branches, leaves, and twigs.

Oscar beamed at her as they drew near, amused to find that everybody was staring at them.

'Helen Fordyce gave you that quilt?' he asked with a twitch of the lips. 'Really, you shouldn't have accepted. It's too much for such a simple gesture.'

'What simple gesture?'

'All in good time.'

'*Now* is a good time!'

'Louise, please,' he begged her, his smile vanishing for an instant. 'Let me introduce my new friend. He's such a remarkable fellow.'

'Come now, Oscar,' he said with a humble bow of the head.

'You've made friends with the druid!' Fay gasped in disbelief.

'How are you, Fay? It's been a while, hasn't it?'

'It certainly has,' she said. 'You never come by this way. You're always stalking through the forest.'

'That's just the way I am, and thankfully so, because that's where I met Oscar. You must be Louise. It's a pleasure to meet you.'

'Likewise,' Louise forced herself to say. For a hermit, he was certainly a charming man. 'You met last night, after the ghost tour?'

'Yes, and then we met up again this morning.'

Oscar winced.

'This morning? But you were asleep when I woke up, and Jane saw you get out of bed just a few minutes ago.'

'Jane saw what I wanted her to see,' he said quietly. 'I suppose I need to explain what's been happening since the ghost tour last night.'

'Yes, you most certainly do!'

'And I will, all in good time, and in an appropriately discreet fashion,' he continued. 'Donald, or the druid, as some of the locals like to call him, has invited us to a well-deserved drink at his caravan.'

'Drink? Isn't it a bit early? I'm just having my coffee.'

'Of course. I'm sorry. I don't know whether it's early or late any longer.'

'It sounds like you've been drinking already!'

'I can assure you that we have been behaving in a very healthy manner this morning. Are you coming or not?'

'All right, I'm coming. Thanks for the coffee, Fay. That was very kind of you.'

'Coffee on the house?' Oscar asked.

Fay nodded.

'And a free patchwork quilt? You're quite the queen of freeloading this morning, my dear!'

#

Donald's caravan was a battered old hulk that had obviously been repaired so many times that little of its original body remained. Sheets of metal had been beaten over parts that had become too corroded to keep the rain out and a wooden lean-to with old vehicle windscreens for windows had been erected on one side. It even had its own garden of herbs and flowers through which they had to pass to get to the door.

'Wonderful!' Oscar announced.

Louise didn't seem so convinced.

'Well, it's home, and I'm comfortable in it,' Donald said.

The ensemble couldn't have been more perfectly hidden. It

was nestled on a flat patch of ground halfway down the hillside between the old hospital and the old post office. The location was so isolated and hard to reach Oscar had to wonder how Donald ever got the caravan there in the first place.

'I can't see where there's a track wide enough for a caravan leading down from the road,' Oscar observed. 'How did you get it here?'

'I didn't. I found it abandoned here and decided to take advantage of it. It seems its previous owner made a mistake and it tumbled all the way down here, which is why it's not exactly in mint condition.'

Donald opened the door to his caravan and a scrawny cat dashed out.

'Go on! Get out of here!'

'Is it yours?' Louise asked.

'Mine? Oh, you know cats. It's mine when it's time for a feed. The rest of the time it belongs to itself.'

The interior of the caravan was far more attractive than the exterior. Donald had all kinds of mystical objects and everyday rubbish piled up on the floor or stacked on the crooked shelves nailed to the walls. There were books all over the place and the smell of cat piss and mildew was partially masked by the overbearing scent of dozens of oils and dried herbs.

Louise pinched Oscar on the arm. He turned around to give her a reassuring glance.

Donald pulled an unmarked bottle out of a filthy looking hessian sack. The green liquid inside it glinted in the filtered sunlight that shone through the caravan's skylight.

'Absinthe?'

'With pleasure,' Oscar replied, rubbing his hands together.

Louise's eyes bulged and she looked at her watch. It wasn't yet eleven o'clock in the morning.

'Not for me, thanks.'

'Rum?'

'I'm fine, thanks.'

Donald shrugged apologetically.

'So, Oscar was telling me about your ghost tour.'

'Yes, have you done it before?'

'No, not me, but I know *all* the stories about the ghosts of Walhalla, and I've seen them. In fact, I see them all the time.'

Donald passed Oscar a glass as he continued.

'But it's not the departed that caused him to creep around the forest last night.'

'Tell her what you told me,' Oscar encouraged him.

Louise didn't think her husband ought to believe a word he said, but she listened politely.

'There was somebody staying up at the old hospital last night.'

'But it's closed for repairs,' Louise said.

'I know that, as does everybody in town. It's been closed down for years now, but its owners don't have the means to pay for the renovations at the moment, so it just sits there, empty.'

'That's what makes it the perfect place to go unnoticed,' Oscar added before emptying his glass.

'Did you go in there last night, after the tour?'

'I was on my way when Donald stopped me.'

They burst out laughing.

'Bloody hell, you gave me the fright of my life!' Oscar said, slapping him on the arm.

'I came straight up out of some bushes by the gate to the hospital and asked him who he was and what his business was sneaking around like that in the middle of the night.'

'And you told him?' she asked Oscar.

'I told him about the sobbing I'd heard and that I wanted to know what was going on, whether it was a ghost or not.'

'And I assured him that it wasn't a ghost,' Donald said. He poured another round of absinthe.

Louise wasn't sure what to think of Donald. He was definitely weird, but was it natural or some kind of act? Oscar seemed to trust him but she didn't know why.

'Do you know who it was then, Donald?'

He shook his head and handed Oscar his glass. Without looking at her, he said, 'I can tell you don't trust me, Louise, and I don't blame you. I'm a weirdo who roams around the valley picking herbs and reading about matters that most people brush off as not being *real*.'

Louise felt a little uncomfortable. She wanted to lie and tell him his impression was wrong.

'Oscar knows I'm not having him on, because I told him what I observed, and as it turns out, our experiences run in parallel. The van, for example; we described it exactly the same way.'

Oscar gulped his absinthe.

'The van?' she asked.

'Sorry, Lou. I didn't get around to telling you.'

'There's a lot you haven't got around to telling me, isn't there? I think it's about time you started!'

'You're right. No need to get angry. I'll tell you. You remember our first night here when we were all alone at the campsite?'

'Yes, I remember. Alone, just like we will be again tonight.'

'Probably,' he agreed. 'Well, I woke up during the night and noticed a van or a small truck, judging by the sound of the motor, heading along the road. It didn't have its headlights on.'

Louise nodded.

'I described the same thing,' Donald continued. 'Except that it was on Friday night. The same night you were attacked by a "ghost" near the old mine entrance where you heard the sobbing. The van came out of the old hospital grounds and continued slowly along the road. I was so surprised that I climbed up to see what was happening, but I got there too late to see the van clearly.'

'What happened next?'

'I followed it along the road, but the driver must have seen me, because it sped off and I couldn't keep up. I decided to go to the old hospital to make sure they hadn't caused any damage.'

'That's when you heard somebody crying?' Louise guessed.

'That's right. But the building's big and I wasn't sure where it was coming from. I walked around the outside and peered in through the windows. There were two figures inside. One was sitting on a bed, and the other, a child, was tucked up in it.'

'Who?' Louise asked.

'I couldn't tell,' he said. 'There was a lamp, and I think the adult was reading to the child.'

'Was it a man or a woman?'

'I couldn't tell.'

'And you could hear the child sobbing?'

'Yes, but then he or she stopped.'

'Could you hear the adult's voice?'

Donald laughed. 'You and your husband are so alike. You both ask precisely the same questions. No, I think the kidnapper was whispering.'

'You believe it's a kidnapping?'

'What else could it be?' Donald asked her.

'But who are the kidnappers, and who is the child, and why?' she asked.

'We don't have all the answers yet,' Oscar said.

'You weren't able to rescue the child?' Louise asked.

'I made a bit of a mistake,' Donald admitted. 'I knocked on the window. I wanted to know who they were and what they were doing there, but the lamp went out and I couldn't see them any longer. By the time I got inside, they'd vanished.'

'Oscar, you inspected the scene?'

'Of course, but there were no clues.'

'Footprints?'

'No, the ground was too hard and dry.'

'That's the second time we've missed our opportunity,' Louise complained. 'We can't afford to mess around when a child's life is at stake.'

Both men nodded.

'But there's a bright side,' Oscar reassured her.

Donald grinned knowingly.

'Well, what is it?'

'I spoke to Michael Stemson from the Star Hotel this morning. Either he or Stephanie drives down to Rawson every morning for supplies, including copies of the daily newspaper.'

'So?'

'He let me read the paper. Wasn't that nice of him?'

'What's that got to do with anything?'

'Come on, Louise. Put two and two together.'

She glared at him.

'Kidnapping…newspaper? I know the child's identity!'

Donald poured him another glass of absinthe.

17.

'You do? In that case, we just need to rescue him or her and call the police.'

'Slow down,' Oscar cautioned. 'We need to find him first, and that has proved difficult thus far. Also, I wouldn't mind knowing why he was kidnapped in the first place.'

'What does that matter?' Louise asked.

'It's of utmost importance,' Oscar replied. 'I can hardly say that I've solved the mystery without knowing who kidnapped the child and why they did it.'

'Does the article give any idea of motive?'

'Unfortunately not. There's a reward for any information leading to the safe return of the child and the arrest of the kidnappers. We don't intend to get in contact with the police until we have all the necessary information.'

'All right,' Louise said. 'What do we know so far?'

'The boy's name is Edward Reinhardt and he's six years old. He was kidnapped from Scotch College.'

'The cap!'

'Precisely. We can suppose it belongs to him and was lost during the hasty transfer from the abandoned mine to the old hospital. As I was saying, he was abducted from just outside the school last Wednesday. He was supposed to be getting a lift home with a friend's mother, but when she arrived, there was no sign of him. As you can imagine, especially for a reputable establishment like Scotch College, the school administration is under intense scrutiny and has been harshly criticised for not enforcing its own strict procedures with regards to the younger students being picked up at the gate.'

'Fair enough!' Louise agreed. 'It's outrageous.'

'Edwards's father, Derrick Reinhardt, is a very wealthy man. He's the CEO of one of the country's biggest coal-mining companies.'

'There was a ransom note?'

'Yes, but there were no specific details in the newspaper.'

'So, the motive is money,' Louise mused. 'That won't help you narrow down the list of suspects.'

'No, it won't. After all, a love of money is the root of all evil.'

'Are any of Walhalla's residents or current visitors strapped for cash?' she asked.

Donald raised his index finger and twisted his wrist until he was pointing straight at himself.

'Anybody else?' she asked.

'Not really. We don't have any particularly wealthy folk here, but nobody is especially poor either.'

'Do you have any ideas?' she asked Oscar.

'I'm afraid not. We can be pretty sure that there are at least two kidnappers and that they have a van. I have a photo of the boot print fragment I found up near the old mineshaft, but, well, that's about all really. If I could find a link between the Reinhardt family and somebody here, it would make things a lot easier. But if the kidnapping was just the opportunistic targeting of the son of a billionaire, it's not going to be so straightforward.'

'What should we do next?'

'We need to tackle both angles. Louise, I'd like you to drive to Rawson or Moe tomorrow and use the internet to do some research into the Reinhardt family. I want you to tell me as much as you can about them.'

'No problem.'

'Donald and I will try to find where Edward is being held captive.'

'When do we start?' Donald asked enthusiastically.

'Let's make it at nightfall. I need some lunch and a long afternoon nap. I think that absinthe is starting to sink in.'

18.

The nap ended up being postponed. Once Oscar and Louise had arrived back at the now empty camping area and opened their tent, he knew immediately that something wasn't quite right.

'Louise, we've had an intruder.'

'Are you sure?'

'There's no doubt about it. I always leave the insect mesh zipper closed at the bottom and now it's at the top.'

'You really do that?'

'Yeah, it's my habit.'

'A habit that you've developed over the last few days?'

'That's right.'

'You're weird.'

'I know.'

'You think the kidnappers know we're on their trail?'

'They must do. Perhaps they overheard us talking to somebody. We've mentioned the sobbing to quite a few people.'

'Yes, and Helen Fordyce knows you're a detective.'

'She does?'

'She guessed. You still have to explain all that business to me.'

'I will, but we need to focus on this first. Let me take a careful look around.'

Louise stood back and watched him display his skills. He walked all around the tent, studying the ground and the tent itself. He touched the insect mesh and rubbed his hands together, then stood up again and looked all around.

'That's interesting,' he said to himself.

'What?'

He showed Louise his fingers.

'What do you call that in English?'

'Sawdust,' he told her. 'Whoever came into our tent had sawdust on his or her hands or clothes.'

'A lot of locals come into contact with sawdust, especially with all the tree lopping going on at the moment,' she reminded him. 'There's sawdust all over the place.'

'I suppose so,' he agreed. 'Hopefully, I'll have more than that to go on.'

He popped back into the tent and moved around very carefully.

'Has anything been stolen?'

'I don't think so. They were probably looking for our cameras or notebooks so that they could find out what we know. I just hope they haven't thrown their hiking boots away. That's about the only piece of solid evidence I have.'

'You still haven't noticed anybody wearing those boots, or my earrings?'

'Wait a minute,' he grumbled. 'Excellent! Look at this!'

He jumped out of the tent triumphantly and held his hand up to Louise with his thumb and index finger pressed firmly together.

'Look at *what*?' She asked him.

'At what I'm holding.'

She took a delicate step as though scared of whatever it might be.

'It won't hurt you. It's just a hair.'

She brought her face up to his hand. He was holding a strand of hair that was neither very long nor very short and was more or less straight.

'I found it caught in the insect mesh.'

She looked at it blankly for a moment.

'It could be anyone's hair,' she said eventually.

Oscar shook his head. 'Not at all. I've only noticed one person in town who has hair that particular colour.'

He watched Louise's face as she stared off into thin air. He could tell she was parading the heads of everybody she'd met in town through her mind's eye.

After a while, she shook her head and shrugged.

'I give up.'

Oscar gave her the name and grinned as her jaw dropped.

19.

Oscar was intent on having that nap. He'd hardly slept at all over the last twenty-four hours and hadn't had a really good night's sleep since arriving in the ghost town. He lay down in the tent and closed his eyes, but instead of falling asleep, his mind raced. He knew who had been in his tent and suspected that person of being involved in the kidnapping. But why?

'Louise, are you there?'

'You should be sleeping,' she called from outside.

'That's a lost cause,' he complained. 'I know I asked you to drive down to Rawson or Moe to do some research tomorrow, but I think today would be better.'

She sighed. The idea of driving all the way down along the winding road that afternoon didn't please her.

'Does Fay have an internet connection?' he asked.

'I don't know. Why do you ask?'

'I thought that maybe you could use her computer. I noticed she had a memory stick on the bunch of keys hanging from her belt.'

'So, you were looking at her arse, were you?'

He laughed. 'Caught red-handed!'

'How do you know we can trust her?'

'Because she didn't have a Yale padlock key hanging from her waist, and because even though she's an irredeemable flirt and is having regular *ménages-à-trois* with Karl and Chelsea Gloz, she's definitely no kidnapper.'

'She's what! Are you serious?'

'Don't get distracted from the matter at hand, honey. I think we can trust her. Can you ask her if you can borrow her computer? We need more information about Derrick Reinhardt.'

'I'm on it!' Louise couldn't believe what she'd just heard but tried to concentrate. 'You need to get some sleep.'

'Afraid not,' Oscar told her. 'I need to talk to Donald right away. There are at least two kidnappers, and I think I know who the other one is, but I can't figure out why they're working together. There must be a reason. Most of all, we still don't know where Edward is being held.'

Oscar unzipped the tent and crawled out, yawning.

'I'll catch up on my forty winks once all this has been cleared up.'

#

Ned and Walt were packing up after a day of tree lopping and burning off. Their chainsaws were already in the tray of the truck and they were busy rolling metal drums across the street when Louise passed them on her way down to The Greyhorse. Smoke from a smouldering fire was rising from the ditch between the road and the creek and spreading out over the town. Ash drifted back down to the ground further away. It wasn't very pleasant and Louise was worried that the tent and her clothes would end up smelling terrible, but the men had a job to do.

'Afternoon,' Ned said as she walked past.

'Finishing up for the day?'

'Yep. Time for a beer or two, I reckon,' he answered enthusiastically.

Walt just gave her a broad grin.

She could sense them both staring at her as she continued down the road. Once she was a little further away, the clanging and thumping started up again as they went back to loading the truck.

When she arrived at The Greyhorse, Fay was drinking an afternoon coffee with Michael, from the Star Hotel, and Gerald Collins. She ordered herself not to let her expression give away the fact that she knew about Fay's dirty little sex life. She wondered whether Michael and Gerald knew about it. The idea made her skin crawl.

'How was your afternoon with the druid?' Fay asked.

The men had a good laugh at that.

'Interesting, to say the least.'

'I bet.'

'Did he show you his caravan?' Gerald asked.

'Yes, he's got some strange stuff in there.'

'Well, you and your husband are quite privileged,' Michael told her. 'None of us ever get invited up there. Not that we would accept anyway.'

'I know he's odd, but he's actually quite a nice man,' Louise said.

'No doubt,' Michael agreed. 'We just like to joke about him. It's just for a harmless laugh.'

'There's bugger all else to laugh about around here,' Gerald added.

'I was just going to close up,' Fay said. 'But I can make you a coffee if you want.'

'Actually, I wanted to ask you a favour.'

'Sure, what is it?'

Louise hesitated.

'In private?' Fay suggested.

'No, it's just that Oscar and I need to check a few things on the internet, but we don't have a connection.'

'Not a problem. Have a seat with the lads while I finish closing up shop, and then I'll take you back to my place.'

'Which means just around the rear of the café,' Michael clarified. 'I've got computers with internet access in a couple of our rooms if you prefer.'

Louise froze, Oscar had said that they could trust Fay, but he hadn't mentioned Michael. Perhaps he was the other kidnapper.

'I really wouldn't feel comfortable doing that. We're not guests at your hotel.'

'You're a guest in my town, and I want to make you feel welcome. I insist!'

Louise found herself nodding. There was no harm in any case. All she had to do was delete the browser's history before leaving and that would cover her tracks, wouldn't it?

'Thank you,' she said.

He finished his coffee and said goodbye to Fay and Gerald.

'Follow me.'

He led Louise to one of the deluxe suites, which came with a widescreen television, an ensuite bathroom, a heavenly looking king-size bed, and a writing desk with a computer.

'I might have to talk Oscar into spending a night here before we leave.'

Michael laughed.

'You knew it, didn't you?'

He nodded.

'You're a clever businessman. All that talk about looking after guests in your town.'

'I meant every word of that,' he said firmly. 'But I must admit I knew you'd succumb to my luxury suite.'

He waved towards the computer.

'Help yourself. There's no password. I'll be downstairs in the bar if you need me.'

Louise waited until he'd closed the door before turning the computer on. She did a search for Derrick Reinhardt and discovered she was going to have to sort through an awful lot of material. There were links to online news publications, social networking websites, and online forum discussions.

One particular theme caught her attention. Derrick Reinhardt, CEO of Fallow Plains Prospecting, wasn't admired and worshipped by all who had crossed his path. He had made himself a host of enemies.

20.

Donald wasn't in his caravan when Oscar got there. They'd arranged to meet at nightfall, so there was a strong possibility that he wouldn't return for a few hours. Oscar walked around his caravan and studied it closely. If the person who'd slipped into his tent was also aware that Donald was working with Oscar, his caravan may have been targeted too.

He tried the door and it swung open with ease. A cloud of concern passed over his face, but remembering that the door hadn't been locked on his previous visits, it soon disappeared. Donald's home was hidden from view, and he owned nothing of great value. He had no reason to keep it locked.

Oscar took a peek inside, just to be safe. Nothing was more

disturbed than usual.

He thought about helping himself to another glass of absinthe, comfortable in the knowledge that his new friend wouldn't have objected had he been there, but decided against it. A few glasses sharpened his mind and opened mysterious and unexpected doorways, but more than a few would render him dull and useless. Edward Reinhardt needed him. He couldn't afford to fail the child.

'Oscar.' Donald's voice made him jump. It was the second time the druid had startled him. The investigator was seldom taken by surprise. He could generally give Louise the name or description of an approaching individual long before any noticeable signs of a stranger's presence had even reached her ears. Donald had a special talent, and it was one that disconcerted Oscar. He could move silently, like an owl or a moth.

'You startled me.'

'Again.'

'How do you move like that?'

'I don't know. I don't walk through the forest, I walk *with* it.'

'Impressive! Now, I have some exciting news to tell you!'

His expression didn't change at all, and Oscar knew there was a problem before he even began to say those unexpected words, 'I know all about it.'

'You do?'

'Yes, I do. Somebody went into your tent while you were with me.'

Oscar suddenly realised that the druid had more talents than he could have possibly imagined.

'I almost started believing in ghosts a few days ago but resisted the temptation. I'm now confronted with a mind reader?'

Donald laughed. 'You should believe in ghosts, but I can't read your mind any more than you can read mine.'

Oscar took that as a challenge. 'I may just be able to read yours.'

'Very well,' Donald said. He stroked his goatee while Oscar considered him.

'Tell me whether I'm right or wrong. You know that one of the kidnappers entered my tent because she told you. It's as simple as that.'

Donald's gaze widened and his hand halted in midstroke.

'Excellent skills of deduction!'

'Thank you,' Oscar said graciously.

'I notice that you said *she* rather than employing the usual masculine third-person pronoun or the trendy gender-neutral third-person plural one for an unknown subject.'

Oscar smiled at his friend. It was like playing a game of chess without the board and pieces. He thoroughly enjoyed a good verbal joust.

'Yes,' he continued. 'That's because I know who it was.'

Donald's jaw dropped.

'How?'

'I'll tell you later.'

Donald frowned.

'And her accomplice?'

'I have my suspicions.'

'But you don't have any solid proof, do you? You couldn't prove that either of them has committed a crime.'

'What's going on here, Donald? Are you tired of living alone in a caravan? Do you want a beautiful house on the coast with the rich vultures, somewhere near Sorrento? Do you want to trade your cat for a gold-digging girlfriend with fake tits?'

'No, I'm happy right here where I am, my friend. I haven't been bought off and I haven't been threatened.'

'In that case, what happened?'

'You're the mind reader, aren't you?'

Oscar closed his eyes and drew a deep breath. Donald was not a man who would sell his principles for money. He, like Oscar, despised such people. The kidnappers, or at least one of them, had spoken to him. Hermit or not, these were locals; people he knew. Bribery, blackmail, menaces, all of that was out of the question. They were on the same wavelength.

'She convinced you that what they were doing was right.'

Donald sighed. He was relieved.

Oscar waited for him to say more.

'She convinced me, Oscar. Yes, indeed. And you know what?'

'You think she would have convinced me too?'

Donald clicked his fingers loudly. 'You're one clever chap, my friend!'

'Kidnapping a child isn't right, regardless of what his father has done.'

'He deserved it!'

'Who? The child?'

'Derrick. He deserved it.'

So, it was personal. Oscar finally knew that for a fact. It wasn't just a random kidnapping. It wasn't simply about money.

'It's not fair on the child. It could traumatise him for life.'

'It might just make him a better person than his father.'

Oscar nodded. Maybe.

'Why did they do it?'

'I promised I wouldn't tell you.'

'We have to release him, Donald. Do you know where he

is?'

'I don't have a clue, and I wouldn't betray a friend even if I did. I'm sorry, Oscar, but you're on your own from here on.'

21.

Louise had found the answer. She read from her notes as they sat at the picnic table next to their tent.

The picture painted of Derrick Reinhardt was one of a horrendously callous man. The unions had taken him to court on several occasions following the injuries and deaths of miners, but his army of lawyers had always got him off the hook. There had been strikes, but they had been broken. He was given bad press, but the return his company's shareholders made on their investment muffled that. He had mountains of money, and he made mountains of money for others. A few accidental deaths caused by cutting back on workplace safety were nothing that couldn't be handled by a man of his influence and standing.

'It's all starting to come together now, Louise. We know why the child was kidnapped.'

'We know more than that,' she teased.

'Did you discover the names of the miners who lost their lives?'

Louise looked him in the eye and nodded slowly, ensuring there was no doubt as to the significance of her findings.

'How about I give you a name?' Oscar suggested, playing her game.

'Before you do that, tell me why you sent me to do research if you'd already solved the case.'

'You're giving me too much credit, honey. I hadn't solved the case. The pieces have only just fallen into place now. What you've told me has cleared up a foggy notion that had been lurking through my mind since somebody said something the other day.'

'Foggy,' she said. 'Very foggy.'

He laughed. 'The point I'm trying to make is that your research is invaluable. Without it, I wouldn't have this name on the tip of my tongue.'

'You know the name, do you?'

'Just the surname.'

'If you're right, you get a kiss, but if you're wrong, I slap that smug face of yours. Deal?'

'Deal,' Oscar said as smugly as possible. 'Are you ready?'

She nodded.

He gave her the name, then puckered his lips.

She swore in French and kissed him.

'I would suggest we take this into the tent,' she whispered, 'but I suppose you're going to have to plan tonight's rescue mission.'

'The hero usually gets the girl after he has saved the day, not before, doesn't he?'

'That's the formula, but I guess we could display a little more originality.'

He looked to the west, where the sun still hovered over the mountains.

'It's far too early for a nocturnal escapade. Let's have a *sieste coquine*.'

Louise grinned. 'I'll try not to wear you out.'

#

Oscar stood under the trees across the street for what seemed like hours, until the bedroom light went out. The glow of the living-room light continued. He guessed that one inhabitant had gone to bed while the other was still up, pretending to read, or absently watching the television; like him, biding time.

Ten minutes later, the light went out and the front door opened. A shadow stepped onto the verandah and paused while it pulled a pair of boots on. Oscar smiled, for he had inspected those boots and checked the pattern of their soles.

The person walked down the few steps that led to the garden path and left the property.

Oscar stayed where he was until there was a safe distance between them, then followed the shadowy form along the main street. The darkness made it difficult at first, but by the time they had arrived at their destination, Oscar had glimpsed enough of the figure to make out black clothes and a bulging balaclava.

The individual unlocked the door, stepped inside, and pushed it closed again.

Oscar didn't hear a deadlock slip into place as he dashed across the street and crept up to the door.

He was in luck. The door wasn't locked. Pushing it ever so delicately, he slipped inside.

On the far side of the shop, beyond an unnerving forest of shadowy statuettes, sculptures, and paintings, a torch was playing on a backroom door and keys were jangling.

The click of a Yale padlock being unlocked cut through the silence, then the figure and the torchlight disappeared as slow shuffling bore witness to an internal staircase.

Oscar took his time manoeuvring along the nearest aisle, making sure not to bump into anything. He peered through the doorway, down the short flight of stairs leading into the basement.

Two voices reached his ears. They were speaking in subdued tones that belied the tension he imagined such a situation would warrant. One of the voices belonged to a boy, and Oscar found the incongruous combination of fear and relief that it revealed rather disquieting. The other voice belonged to a woman. She spoke in soothing tones, and Oscar listened from the top of the staircase, eager to hear what would be said. The child no longer uttered a word. The woman's voice was rising and falling rhythmically, with pauses here and there.

Even before Oscar descended into the basement, he knew what he would find—a woman wearing a balaclava, reading her prisoner a bedtime story.

He removed the padlock from the door, as a precaution, and walked down the stairs.

She looked up from the book and gasped.

'Don't panic,' he said softly as they caught sight of him. The basement was small and rough, probably as old as the town itself, but the mattress and bedding they sat on looked comfortable. There was a portable toilet, and an old shelf bore an array of toys, books, tools, and utensils.

'You!' the woman said.

Oscar nodded. 'It ends tonight.'

'You know who I am?' she asked.

'No,' he lied, and she immediately understood what he was doing. 'Whoever you are, go straight home and stay there.'

'Can I trust you?'

'You need to do what I say.'

Without another word, she slipped past him and up the stairs.

'How are you going, young man?'

He burst out crying. 'I want to go home!'

'You will, very soon, but first you need a hot shower and some hot chocolate.'

That brought a smile to his lips. 'What's your name?'

'You can call me Shane. What's yours?'

'Edward.'

'You're safe now, Edward. Do you know where you are?'

He shook his head.

'I'm going to get you back to your family, but you need to trust me. Can you do that?'

'I think so.'

22.

Once Fay had recovered from her initial shock, she was only too glad to look after Edward until his return home could be arranged. She went along with Oscar's plan, despite the scanty details he was willing to provide. No names were given, and there was no explanation offered as to why he insisted on calling her Jessica. Nor was it clear why Oscar had whispered into her ear, specifying that the boy wasn't to come into contact with any maps or materials of any kind mentioning the name of the town or to leave her home. He was placing his trust in her, and she was placing hers in him.

Oscar hurried down the street to Tainsh Cottage and wasn't surprised to find a van parked out front and a lamp on in the living room.

He stepped onto the verandah and noticed the tell-tale boots back beside the front door. He was about to knock when he realised the door had been left slightly ajar. It was a thoughtful gesture considering the circumstances, and the possibility of it being a trap had no sooner entered his mind than it departed.

The door creaked as he pushed it open, and a familiar voice

called to him. 'Come in, Oscar. May I call you Oscar?'

He stepped into the living room. 'You may, Andrea,' he replied, doing his best to exude dignity, reassurance, and reasonableness.

Sitting together on a sofa were Andrea and Deirdre, worry written on their faces. Gerald was sitting apart, on a worn leather armchair. He was clearly both upset and confused.

'Oscar,' Andrea pleaded. 'Tell my dear husband I haven't been cheating on him. He has got it into his mind that I've been crawling into another man's bed at night, though whose it could be in this ghost town is beyond me.'

'Is he ready for the truth?'

'He needs to hear it, whether he's ready or not,' she admitted.

Oscar sat on a padded chest and looked from Andrea to Deirdre. 'I'm not the one who ought to break the news. It should be you, Andrea, or your sister.'

The women shot each other a glance.

'You would be surprised how well I've come to know Walhalla and its inhabitants. By the way, Deirdre, your van has a blown brake light. You really ought to replace the bulb.'

She shifted uncomfortably.

'Let's cut to the chase, Andrea,' Gerald snapped, clearly unappreciative of Oscar's skills. 'What the hell has been going on?'

'Listen, darling, you might want to pour us all a drop of whisky,' she told him. 'We need to toast our sorely missed son before I confess.'

The whisky went down well, much better than Andrea's revelation, but rather than losing his temper, Gerald grew sullen.

'You're a private investigator, Oscar. You have no

connection to the police. Is that right?'

'That's correct.'

'I'm sure you can understand my wife's foolish mistake. We're not wealthy people, but we have some savings.'

Oscar held his hand up, and Gerald held his tongue.

'In my experience, some words are best left unspoken,' Oscar said. 'Likewise, some transactions are best left unmade. All I want is for this boy to be returned home as discreetly as possible, and for these two women to renounce their interest in criminal careers. *Thelma and Louise* looks like a lot of fun on the big screen, but the reality is an altogether different matter.'

23.

'Well, that didn't end up being the relaxing holiday I was after, but I guess that's how it is with Oscar Tremont in the equation,' Louise mused while they packed their tent away. 'You cracked the case, as usual, but you've failed in one regard.'

'What's that?'

She tugged her bare earlobes.

Oscar smiled cheekily, making his moustache twitch, and reached into a pocket.

'My earrings!'

'Failed in one regard, you say?'

'It was Deirdre, wasn't it? That strand of auburn hair was hers.'

'Yes, it was her hair, and, yes, she came into our tent, but she wasn't the thief.'

'Who was it?'

'Try changing that *who* to a *what* and you'll be a step closer.'

'An animal stole them?'

'I found them in a nest along the Tramline Walkway, along with a beer bottle cap, some Christmas tinsel, a chocolate bar wrapper, and a silver hairpin Helen Fordyce inherited from her mother. The culprit was a bowerbird.'

'A bowerbird,' she repeated. 'A bowerbird took my earrings and stole Helen's hairpin. That's what the quilt was all about. It was payment in kind.'

'While I was talking to her, I mentioned your earrings, and she told me about her hairpin. That got me thinking.'

'You guessed what had happened and climbed around in the trees trying to find my earrings for me?'

Oscar was about to reply, but she kissed him passionately, smothering his words.

'I didn't have to climb, Louise. Bowerbirds build their nests on the ground.'

'They do? Rather considerate thieves, aren't they?'

Oscar laughed as she got in the car. They were both ready to bid Walhalla farewell.

The Witch at the Window

Prologue

The last few stragglers were tramping back through the dunes and trying to locate their tents and cabins in the dark. The day had been sunny and the evening pleasant, but clouds had swept in from the sea just after midnight, smothering the moon and stars. Only the bobbing red and green lights of distant beacons and the flicker of a fire further along the beach interrupted the obscurity that cloaked the Tallebudgera caravan park.

'Can we talk?' she asked once they were alone on the beach.

'I had a feeling this was coming,' he replied, a bitter edge to his voice. 'You've been distant all weekend.'

'I know. I've been waiting for the right time.' Her words were slurred.

'What happened? I don't know what I've done.'

'It's not you, it's…' she paused. Even her drunken mind recognised that she was about to spout a cliché.

He finished it for her.

'Sure, it's me…you…whatever.'

'You're fun to be around, but, well, we're just not in love, are we?'

He pulled two more beers out of his backpack.

'One last drink together?' he pleaded.

She smiled and nodded, then looked out towards the surf. She didn't notice him slip something into one of the bottles before handing it to her.

'Cheers,' he said, his voice and expression demonstrating a mature reaction to the situation. After all, getting dumped is just part of growing up.

They drank in silence for a while, until he could tell the drug was kicking in. He'd been told the first stage was euphoria—the highest of all highs.

'Let's go for a walk,' he suggested.

But she had other ideas. 'I'll race you to the waves!' she challenged him.

Then she was up on her feet and running.

He soon overtook her and caught her just as they reached the water.

'Let's swim for a while,' he said.

She didn't reply. Her head was spinning from the drug and exertion.

He grabbed her by the hand and pulled her further out into the surf. Waves were breaking over them, slamming them down, and for a moment it was all confusion and tumbling.

A minute later, he staggered out of the water and headed back towards the dunes. He looked up and down the beach and felt sure that he was alone.

He was wrong. A scream ripped through the night air.

He froze momentarily, and then hurried over the dune and back to his cabin. Inside, it was as dark as a whale's belly and filled with loud snoring.

'Help! Help!' echoed through the night, and the voice was soon joined by a chorus of others. People were asking what was going on. Somebody shouted that it was coming from the beach.

But inside the cabin, nobody stirred. Their sleep was too deep.

He crept over to his bed and crawled under the sheets.

1.

Oscar Tremont was in the middle of his morning jog along Enoggera Creek when his phone rang. He got off the pathway, drew to a stop under the branches of the mangroves that grew on the creek bank, and pulled the phone out of the right-hand pocket of his track pants.

He had assumed it would be his wife, Louise. She sometimes called after she'd left for work to remind him to buy toilet paper or to check that she'd switched the iron off. But he didn't recognise the number displayed on the screen.

'A client?' he asked himself before accepting the call.

His eyebrows rose as he listened to the caller.

'Yes, I know who you are, Mr Weldon. May I ask how you heard about my services?'

Lorikeets were squabbling in the mangroves, and further down the pathway, two dogs barked at each other aggressively, ignoring their owners' demands for calm. Oscar couldn't hear the caller very well, but when he heard the words *stolen Porsche*, he understood.

'Ah, yes. Your friend was very pleased that I succeeded in finding his car. He was less pleased with the uselessness of the police and with the company his son was keeping.'

Oscar had an instinctive dislike for the filthy rich, but work was quiet and he needed money.

'Mr Weldon…very well, *Rod*…how can I be of assistance?'

He checked for cyclists and joggers before crossing the path to get away from the noisy lorikeets. He stopped next to a frame holding three chin-up bars.

'Five o'clock is fine. My address is 13 Dover Street, Wilston. Please bring any documents or photographs that could help me with your problem…Yes…All right, see you this evening then, Rod.'

Oscar ended the call and put his phone away.

Rod Weldon, media magnate and one of the wealthiest men in broadcasting in Queensland. He hadn't wanted to explain himself over the phone, but his voice had conveyed his distress. Blackmail? Likely. Suspected extramarital affair? Hopefully not, for although that kind of case was easy money, it wasn't intellectually stimulating.

Oscar did three sets of chin-ups and jogged back home. After a warm shower and some breakfast, he would get started finding out as much as he could about Rod Weldon.

#

Oscar was on the verandah, sitting on his thinking chair, when a Jaguar pulled up at the kerb. The man who got out was in his fifties and was quite handsome despite being a bit podgy around the waist. He certainly looked better in person than in the various newspaper shots Oscar had found online.

Oscar went to the front gate, not only to welcome his client, but also to check that he hadn't been followed. Satisfied the coast was clear, he greeted Rod Weldon and shook his hand. The media magnate's grip was firm, but his frown of concern and look of fatigue bore witness to his true state.

'Come inside, Rod. Would you like a cup of tea or coffee? Or maybe a dram of scotch to calm your nerves?'

Rod struggled to crack a smile. 'Oh, a nip of scotch would do the trick!' he exclaimed. 'Trick,' he repeated to himself quietly. 'Poor bloody choice of words.'

Oscar's eyes narrowed. 'Hold that thought, Rod. Hold that thought! I'll be back in an instant. Take a seat.'

The investigator dashed inside, the word that had so haunted his client echoing through his head.

Someone is playing a trick on him?

Oscar emerged with two glasses of Lagavulin. He handed one to Rod and said cheers, before lowering himself onto his thinking chair.

'Trick?' Oscar asked.

Rod nodded. He had the air of a man who was sure of himself under normal circumstances. His dark grey suit was expensive and the diamond-encrusted pin he wore on his silk tie told the tale of a man who had money and wanted others to know it.

'I've never been a superstitious man, Oscar, but in recent weeks, I've had to reassess that. I'm told you investigate matters that the police wouldn't even touch, affairs of the...' he had to force himself to utter the words, 'supernatural kind.'

Oscar sipped at his scotch and hummed. 'I have indeed. However, in each case, the seemingly supernatural cause turned out to be very much human in nature.'

'Let me put it bluntly, Oscar. I have been hexed.'

'Hexed?' Oscar had to admit to himself that he'd failed to predict the problem.

'Yes, by a witch.'

'By a witch,' Oscar repeated. 'Naturally.'

Rod Weldon stared at the investigator, almost daring him to laugh in his face. But Oscar was taking him seriously.

'Tell me *everything*, from the beginning. I want to hear every detail, no matter how insignificant it may seem.'

Rod drank a nip of scotch, then drew a deep breath.

'It all started three weeks ago. Let me set the scene. I live near Mount Coot-tha, at the top of a long dead-end street. The house next to mine has been empty for almost a year now. Neighbours have told me the owners are overseas, but they've always kept to themselves, so I don't know much about them. What I do know, even though my own wife and son refuse to believe me, is that I have seen a woman at the window of that house, looking down onto my property.'

Oscar felt a shiver of delight. This was a mystery he was going to thoroughly enjoy. 'Go on,' he encouraged.

'Well, it shook me up,' Rod admitted. 'It's really got me rattled. I mean, at first, I just thought she might have been a friend or relative of the owners who was staying there. But I only see her once every few days, and it's always at that same window, looking down into my back yard, where I have a large terrace with a pool built on a steep slope.'

'Can you describe her?'

'Yes, well, not easily. She wears a veil over her face, a kind of black lace veil, and her clothes are strange and colourful, like a gypsy or a bohemian. She stands there very still and only moves her hands in an unsettling way.'

'You think she's casting a spell on you?' Oscar ventured.

'She is. I know she is. I've never believed in magic before, but that's the only explanation. She's using black magic on me, and I don't know why!'

'Calm down, Rod. I'll get to the bottom of this. That's what I do. It seems to me that whoever this is wants to drive you mad. You mustn't let that happen. Do you understand? This person must think the scheme is working, and you need to play along with that, but you mustn't let it actually work.'

Rod nodded. 'It is a witch though, Oscar. It's a real witch!'

'What has happened?'

'I've seen her three times, and each time, something horrible has happened soon afterwards. The first time I saw her at the window, about three weeks ago, my roses died the next day. They *all* died, six rose plants, overnight. I asked my gardener about it and he told me they'd been poisoned, but nobody could have done that. Nobody can get onto the terrace without coming through the front door and through the house.'

Oscar nodded, but he didn't agree. Rich people always overestimated the security of their homes. It was a psychological defence mechanism.

'The second time I saw her, the following week, my toilets clogged up. It took a plumber several days to fix the problem.'

Oscar suppressed a smirk.

'The third time, we were infested with rats, hundreds of them. My wife was away on business, thank goodness, otherwise she would have run screaming all the way down the street.'

'You say that your wife doesn't believe you?'

'No. Look, there's no point pretending, Oscar. We don't get along too well. We don't see much of each other, and it's better that way. She was home when the roses died but she just told me the gardener must have done it on purpose and that I ought to fire his arse. He's an excellent gardener though, and he has no reason to want to sabotage my roses. It makes no sense.'

Oscar closed his eyes for a moment. 'I have to admit, Rod, this is quite possibly the most bizarre mystery I've ever been asked to solve.'

'Is that a *yes*?'

'It most certainly is,' Oscar confirmed. 'Do you have a spare room in your house?'

Rod smiled. '*A* spare room. I've got a few.'

'Good. I'll need to be on the ground and ready to act if I'm going to solve this affair.'

'No problem. What should I tell my family?'

'Let's pretend I'm an old friend from college.'

'Great idea,' Rod agreed. 'I guess we should get our story straight then?'

'As an arrow,' Oscar answered.

2.

Oscar left a note for Louise explaining that he wouldn't be at home much over the coming days and giving an outline of his disguise as Rod Weldon's old friend, Richie Beale. If she called him, he would answer in keeping with his role. Once he had done that, Rod drove him through Ashgrove and Bardon to his home near Mount Coot-tha.

The magnate's home was, as he had said, perched on a mountainside, near the end of a cul-de-sac. There was just one other house further along—the witch house. All the houses in the street were on the right-hand side, which was the lower side as one travelled up towards the end. Their entrances were at street level and their living quarters were propped up over a steep descent at the back. The upper side of the street was covered in dense woodland, for the time being. Oscar didn't imagine it would be long before it was opened up to the luxury property market.

Rod Weldon's home was protected by high white walls and little of the residence itself was visible from the street. He pressed a button on the remote controller fixed to his car's steering wheel and one of three garage doors began to roll upwards. Once he'd parked and Oscar had grabbed his duffel bag, they passed through a door leading to the front garden. A path of smooth stones cut through a strip of white pebbles stretching from the boundary wall to the Weldon family home. The house was essentially three huge white blocks stuck awkwardly together. To Oscar, it seemed like the work of a giant toddler.

Rod punched in a code to open the front door. Oscar memorised it and then glanced along the walls and around the front portico, making a mental note of the location of the security cameras. They had been installed in a logical and professional manner, but any burglar worth his salt would be able to navigate his way through the front garden without being filmed.

Rod led him inside and through to the living room.

'Would you like a glass of Perrier?'

'Yes, thank you.'

Oscar strolled over to the rear of the living room, which was made up of glass sliding doors that gave access to the terrace. There was a swimming pool, barbecue equipment, and several deck chairs. Up against the low wall at the edge of the terrace were six dead rose bushes. He saw treetops beyond the terrace, indicating just how far the drop was. In the distance, the skyscrapers of the city centre and the islands of Moreton Bay could be glimpsed.

'May I look outside?'

'Of course. Tell me if you see her,' Rod replied.

Oscar slid one of the doors open and stepped onto the terrace. To the left, on slightly higher ground, an older but equally expansive mansion loomed. It was imitation Tudor with black and white walls and a roof of terracotta tiles. The window from which Rod had been hexed was the only one visible. It seemed innocent enough, reflecting blue sky and green leaves.

Oscar studied everything carefully and checked his view of the window from every possible angle. He inspected the roses. Obviously, Rod hadn't asked his gardener to replace them, presumably because he was worried he would further anger the witch if he took steps to undo her hex.

Rod joined him outside, glancing at the window as he approached Oscar. 'No sign of her? It's safe to drink the water then,' Rod said, smiling uncomfortably as he handed Oscar a glass.

Oscar knelt and looked at the soil around the roses.

'There were no footprints,' Rod said. 'Nobody can get onto this terrace without coming through the house.'

'I see,' Oscar replied, but he had already noted three ways a trespasser with a certain level of fitness and the right tools could climb onto the terrace from the rear or either of the neighbouring properties.

Making sure his back was facing the window of the adjacent house, he slipped a small plastic container from his pocket and filled it with soil from around the base of one of the rose bushes.

Then, standing up, he asked Rod, 'What did your plumber tell you had happened when your toilets clogged up?'

Rod looked up at the window again before taking a sip from his glass of Perrier, then he walked over to the edge of the terrace and waved his hand casually in the direction of the trees.

'He said that a root had most likely cracked the pipe and ended up blocking it.'

Dozens of eucalypts grew on the mountainside. Smaller trees, bushes, and wild grass covered the ground between them. A stretch of street and the roofs of houses could be made out a hundred metres or so downhill.

'When was this place built?' Oscar asked.

'Sixteen years ago. We are only its second occupants,' Rod answered, then he realised what Oscar was getting at. 'So, you think the plumber was wrong?'

'Well, I'm no plumber,' Oscar said, 'but it seems to me that it takes a long time for roots to disrupt sewage pipes. Sixteen years? Maybe,' he mused. 'I don't know. You no longer have any problem with the toilets?'

'No.'

'But he didn't go down into the yard and identify the precise cause of the problem?'

'No, I don't think so. I really can't say. I wasn't here with him.'

'You didn't mention the witch?'

'No, I didn't. Just imagine what would have happened if word got out that Rod Weldon thought he was being spooked by a witch!'

'I wonder how a witch could block your pipes.'

Rod shook his head. 'I don't know, Oscar. I wish I did.'

'There are no steps leading down from the terrace. How do you get into the back yard?'

'Through the house,' Rod explained. 'There is an internal staircase that leads down to a door under the terrace. It's a bit of a squeeze. We don't go down there much.'

'Is it all right if I snoop around down there for a while?'

'Not at all. Follow me.'

Rod took Oscar back into the house and down a short staircase between the kitchen and the laundry. They stooped as they went out through a doorway and under the terrace.

'Do you always keep this door locked?'

'Always, and like I said, we almost never come down here.'

Oscar looked at the ground near the door. It was hard and

dry, not the kind of soil that would yield footprints. The pool pump stood on a concrete pedestal but there was nothing else to be found under the terrace.

'I've got a few calls to make, I'm afraid. Can I leave you to it? I'll help you get settled in later on.'

'Of course, go ahead. I'll let you know if I need anything.' And with that, Oscar strolled downhill, observing and analysing everything around him.

3.

Helen Weldon arrived home just before half past six that evening and was in such a hurry to pack her bags for her flight the next day that Rod and Oscar barely had a chance to put the college friend story into effect.

'This is Richie Beale, an old friend from college. He's going to stay for a couple of nights,' Rod said, and Oscar was impressed by his flawless lying. It must have been part of his media training.

'Nice to meet you, Ricky,' she said without even a hint of enthusiasm.

Neither Oscar nor Rod bothered to correct her.

'Sorry to be rude but I'm in a bit of a fluster. I have to get ready to fly to Sydney tomorrow and I've got a da…dinner appointment tonight. I'm sure Rod will make you feel at home though.'

She kicked her high heels off and disappeared upstairs.

'*That* is my wife,' Rod said quietly.

'She keeps herself busy,' Oscar ventured.

'She does indeed. We try to keep out of each other's hair.' He took a step closer and whispered, 'Once she has left, we'll be able to speak freely together.'

'You told me earlier that Steve lives with you. Is that right?'

'Yes, he does. But he's not often at home. He's studying at the University of Queensland, doing a degree in electrical engineering. I give him a generous allowance in accordance with his results, and he makes sure he spends every cent of it.' He lowered his voice again. 'Helen doesn't know, but we're having a big party this weekend while she's out of town.'

Oscar grinned, causing his moustache to curl cheekily. Rod Weldon was turning out to be a confusing mix of cynical businessman, mischievous playboy, and superstitious old man. Before meeting earlier that evening, Oscar had known little about the media magnate other than what he'd heard through news reports broadcast by the ABC, and based on that, his opinion of him hadn't been very high. Now, here in the man's home, he was learning about his private life and his psychological state, and he disliked the man even more. He seemed friendly enough, but he lived in a different world from Oscar's, one ruled by a different set of values.

'If you haven't caught the witch in the meantime,' Rod whispered, 'you'll be here for the big night. That's not an invitation to take your time though.'

'On that subject,' Oscar said. 'I need to ask you whether you're happy for me to take a particular approach. I'll explain once your wife has left.'

Rod just shrugged his shoulders and said, 'Let's have another glass of scotch. I've got a bottle of Glenfarclas 30 that a man like you is bound to appreciate.'

'I've always wanted to try that drop.' Oscar's opinion of Rod Weldon suddenly went up a notch.

'I don't have anything for dinner tonight, but there's a really good Indian restaurant in Rosalie. I'll have them deliver a couple of curries.'

'Sounds great,' Oscar said. 'I notice you have a chess set,' he added, pointing at a shelf beside the widescreen television. 'Do you play?'

'I'm not very good,' Rod admitted.

'That doesn't matter. It's just that chess helps me think, and if we play on the terrace, it'll enable me to discreetly observe the witch house.'

'Oh, right. Well, I'll let you set the board up. There's a cane table out there between the deck chairs, as I'm sure you've already noticed. I'll bring the drinks out in a minute.'

He switched an external light on. It lit the terrace like a stadium.

'Is there any way you can dim the light?' Oscar asked.

'Yes, of course,' Rod replied. 'We don't want steal the show, assuming there's to be one tonight.'

Oscar took the chess set from the shelf, glancing at the other items around it as he picked it up. There were family photos of Rod, Helen, Steve, and a girl who was presumably their daughter, as well as books, mostly biographies of television personalities. He stepped outside, set the board up, and sat on the deck chair facing the window. He glanced up. The house was dark inside.

The scotch was so glorious Oscar decided he would thank his client by letting him win the first game. As they were setting the board up for a second, Helen came downstairs and rushed out the front door without so much as waving goodbye.

'What I was going to ask you,' Oscar asked quietly, just in case the witch really was nearby, 'is whether you would have a problem with me inspecting the house.'

'That house?' Rod asked, pointing at himself to indicate behind him.

Oscar nodded and made his opening move.

'I don't understand. I don't have a key. I'm not in contact with the owners.'

'I don't need a key,' Oscar told him.

'You want to break in?'

'*Break in* sounds rather crude. I'd like to *gain access*.'

'Illegally.'

'In this world of ours, a great deal of evil is perpetrated legally, and a great deal of good could be achieved illegally. I'm going to have a hard time solving this mystery if I can't find out what's happening on the other side of that pane of glass.'

'What if she's in there?'

'She won't catch me. The case depends on that.'

'Fine,' Rod said. 'Just be careful.'

'You're the one who ought to be careful,' Oscar replied as he took a rook.

Rod smiled.

'Leave it to me. In the morning, I'll let you know what I've discovered.' Oscar frowned. 'But if I'm not here for breakfast, I want you to burn that house to the ground.'

Rod stared at him wide-eyed. Oscar wasn't joking.

4.

Oscar sat at the window of the guest room he'd chosen as his sleeping quarters for the duration of the case. The room was spacious and comfortable and had an ensuite bathroom, but he had chosen it for its window, which provided a clear view and ease of access.

He heard Steve arrive just before midnight, but for the past hour, the night had been quiet, and he'd witnessed no activity other than the comings and goings of bats and possums.

'Time for some nocturnal ambulation before you fall asleep,' Oscar said to himself, getting up from his chair. He was already dressed for action in a black tracksuit, a utility belt around his waist, a camera and a torch around his neck, and a black beanie covering his shaven head.

He pulled a rope with evenly spaced knots along its length from his duffel bag and tied one end to a heavy chest at the foot of his bed. He removed two towels from the chest and placed them where the rope would touch the frame of the window. Then, with a quick glance at the neighbour's window and down at the terrace to ensure the coast was still clear, he opened the window and lowered the rope.

It only took him a few seconds to dash across the terrace, fling himself over the side wall, and land almost silently on the ground directly beneath the window. He flicked his torch on, keeping it close to the ground so as to minimise stray light and allow him to identify any clues, then crept around the corner of the house and up the brick staircase at the back. At the top, he looked all around. A cool breeze brushed his face and tickled the hairs of his moustache. It made the leaves of the trees that stood sentry in the steep yard whisper secretively.

Confident that he remained undetected, Oscar turned his attention to the back door. It was a simple wooden affair and its lock wouldn't have given him any trouble, but he immediately saw that no picking would be required. A sticky substance was jammed between the edge of the door and the frame. It was the first time the investigator had seen anything of the kind, but its purpose was obvious; to keep the door closed and give the impression that it was locked whilst allowing it to be opened and closed easily with minimal noise.

He was impressed. It wasn't magic, but it was certainly tricky. It also helped him imagine the kind of individual he was dealing with. Clues would be scarce, if not non-existent, and he would need to tread very carefully.

He switched his torch off and used one gloved hand to gently turn the doorknob and the other to apply measured pressure to the door. He slipped inside and closed the door behind him, then waited in silence for ten seconds before flicking the torch back on and sweeping it around the kitchen. He inspected the stove, basin, and the refrigerator, which was switched off and empty. Then he moved into the room to his left. It was a side room full of bookshelves. This was where the window was located.

He switched his torch off again, then stepped over to the window and looked out. The view was as he had expected. Every inch of Rod's terrace could be seen from there. His rope seemed to be crawling up the wall towards the guest room window like a monstrous carpet snake.

Oscar tried to put himself in the position of the witch, both physically and mentally. He stared at Rod's terrace.

But if there were answers to be found, they would most likely to be right there in that room, behind the window. He drew the curtains closed, telling himself not to forget to open them before he left, switched his torch on again, and set about studying the side room.

The bookshelves were dusty, as were parts of the floor. He used that dust to tell him a story, but the details remained vague. There was an armchair to one side of the window. He looked at it carefully and used a pair of tweezers and a sandwich bag from his utility belt to collect three long, blonde hairs caught in the fabric. He pulled the cushion up, but it was clean underneath. To the other side of the window, there was a coffee table with a lamp on it. The lamp had a veil of thin, red material draped over it. Other than that, the table was clean—

clean, not dusty, Oscar noted.

After investigating the entire house, he had to admit that although he had learned a great deal about the owners, he had discovered very little about the witch at the window. He left with just three strands of hair that may or may not have belonged to the suspect.

He smiled to himself as he climbed the rope back into the guest room. He had wanted a mystery worthy of his talents.

5.

Oscar got up early in the morning. Rod was making coffee when he went downstairs, and his son was on his laptop.

'Richie, this is my son, Steve,' Rod said. 'I've told him all about you.'

'Nice to meet you, Steve.'

'Hi,' Steve replied, barely looking up.

'Look, I've got to run. You'll be right?'

'Absolutely. I've got a thing or two to get done today.'

'I'll leave you the code for the front door,' Rod said.

Oscar didn't tell his client he'd already memorised it.

'Did you have a good night's sleep?'

'Very satisfying,' Oscar answered, understanding what his client had really meant.

Rod smiled as he poured a cup of coffee for himself. Oscar could tell that his presence was making the magnate feel more at ease. He had confidence in his abilities, and Oscar was eager not to disappoint.

He scribbled the code on a scrap of paper and pointed at it for Oscar's benefit, before taking a sip of his coffee and saying, 'I'm afraid I've got to run now.'

'See you later, Rod.'

Once Rod was gone, he decided to get some information out of Steve.

'You're looking forward to your party?'

'Yeah,' Steve replied. 'Are you going to be here for it?'

Oscar got the distinct impression the lad was hoping he'd say that he wouldn't be.

'I'm not sure yet. Coffee?'

'No, thanks.'

Oscar poured himself a cup.

'How many people are coming?'

'Forty or fifty. It should be pretty good. It's themed—people and creatures of the sea.'

'I see.' Oscar's mind started cranking. 'Has the party been planned for a while?'

'Yeah,' Steve said, frowning at the strange question but still looking at his laptop. 'I don't know. I announced it three or four weeks ago and invited a few friends.'

A few friends? Oscar couldn't think of forty or fifty people with whom he'd like to spend an evening. He wanted to ask Steve to tell him about each of the people he'd invited, but that would have been stretching the questioning too far. There was one thing Oscar was willing to bet on—that the witch would make an appearance during the party. What he wasn't so sure of was that he would get a chance to see her before then. He hoped he would. He wanted to have some idea what was behind the whole affair before the party kicked off.

6.

By the time Rod arrived that evening, Oscar had filled in a number of blanks regarding the mysterious happenings at the magnate's mansion. All it had taken was a whole lot of snooping and meditating.

They were alone in the house and Oscar was glad to be able to drop the college friend routine and speak plainly to his client.

'You ought to have a drink alone this evening,' he told Rod. 'The witch is more likely to make an appearance if she thinks there's nobody else around.'

'Fair enough,' Rod said. 'Where will you be?'

'I'll keep watch from the bedroom window.'

'Let's do it then.' Rod went over to the fridge and grabbed a beer. On his way back, he took a copy of The Financial Times from the kitchen counter. He walked outside and stretched out on a deck chair, facing the window.

Oscar made himself a cup of herbal tea and hurried upstairs to his bedroom. It felt ridiculous, and he knew he may very well have been wasting his time, but he held fast.

The sun soon began its descent behind the mountain. Before long, if Rod was going to continue reading the paper, he would have to turn the outside light on.

As it turned out, that wouldn't be necessary.

At twenty past six, a red glow lit the witch window and made Oscar jump.

A woman stepped into view.

What struck Oscar most about her was that she didn't fit the stereotype of the wicked witch. There was no pointed hat, crooked nose, or broomstick. She wore a black veil and a flowing dress that would have been white if not for the scarlet lamplight.

He raised his binoculars and studied her in detail. He tried to see her hair but couldn't because the veil covered her head entirely. The only part of her body that was visible was from the base of her neck to her cleavage. Her breasts swelled as she breathed.

'Leave me alone!' Rod yelled, leaping out of his deck chair and sending The Financial Times fluttering into the pool. 'What have I done to deserve this?'

The witch's hands came into view. She wore rings on every finger and her nails were the dark red of fortified wine.

She shook her hands as she brought them slowly up until they reached the veil. Holding it gingerly with the index finger and thumb of each hand, she lifted it up just enough to expose her mouth.

'Please!' Rod's voice was pleading now.

Her lips parted slowly, sensually, and froth poured out of her mouth and down her chin. It cascaded onto her breasts and into her cleavage, soaking her dress and making the thin fabric cling to her nipples.

She titled her face towards the ceiling and held her arms up, then swayed from side to side and slowly sank until she disappeared from view, as though swallowed by the floor.

A moment later, the light went out.

'Oscar! Where are you?' Rod shouted.

The investigator was already rushing down the stairs leading to the door under the terrace. He was planning on dashing into the back yard and observing the witch's flight downhill, but she was faster than he had expected and he saw her disappear into the gloom of the trees.

He sprinted after her and stumbled along a faint track that led downhill. He almost tripped on rocks and roots, but managed to stay on his feet.

Just before he reached the wire fence that marked the boundary, he heard a car engine start up. He glanced to his left but found his view blocked by trees, even when he peered over the fence. He then saw a blue Ford Fiesta with spots of rust on its roof accelerate along the street. A girl with long blonde hair was at the wheel. She didn't notice him.

He tried to catch the registration number, but the angle and the gathering gloom made that impossible. All he could do was watch the car speed away.

7.

Oscar's alarm went off at six o'clock on Saturday morning. He'd set it before going to bed, just after calling Louise, because he'd wanted to get up before Rod and Steve. He scribbled a note and left it on the kitchen bench, just beside the coffee machine. It explained that he had a couple of leads to follow and that it would be best for him to arrive inconspicuously at the party, once there was already quite a crowd there. They were both valid points, and not untrue, strictly speaking, but he failed to mention the main reason for his absence, which was simply that he wanted to have a weekend breakfast with his wife. It would have been nice to surprise her, but she had the car, so he had arranged for her to meet him at a café within walking distance of the mansion.

Rod discovered the note half an hour later and wasn't concerned in the slightest. He was determined to enjoy a quiet morning coffee or two and then wake Steve up when it was time to get to work. They had a busy day ahead.

Rod drank his coffee on the deck, staring defiantly at the window. Oscar had asked him about his enemies, and he had given the question a lot of thought, but he couldn't for the life of him think of anyone who would try to get at him in such a theatrical way. The people who were jealous of him or who may have felt that he had wronged them were conventional and unimaginative types.

After his second coffee, Rod took his T-shirt off, chased all thought of curses from his mind, and hopped into the pool. He floated around, not wanting to exert himself too much with a stomach full of coffee. He tried to resist the temptation to even glance at the window, but he couldn't help himself. He looked again and again. Each time, it was exactly the same, glass reflecting a clear morning sky. As ridiculous as the notion was, its refusal to change affronted him. He was conscious that it was absurd to feel mocked by the window's intransigence. The witch, in the time he'd seen her there—which added up to a matter of seconds—had made that inanimate object an instrument of perpetual distress.

He drew a breath, closed his eyes, and let himself sink into the cool water. It was another world down there, silent and safe, but the tranquillity was short-lived. A dull explosion echoed around him, and even before the pulse of water enveloped his body, he realised he was no longer alone in the pool. Somebody, or something, was with him. He pushed his feet against the pool floor with all his might and rocketed up into the air, his waist clearing the surface. He opened his eyes and looked around as he came back down. There was nobody.

In an instant, he was climbing out of the pool, and it was then that Steve emerged from below the surface. He'd dived in one end and swum underwater towards the other.

'Bloody hell!' Rod bellowed.

Steve shook his head to get the water out of his ears and looked wide-eyed at his dad. 'What's wrong?'

Rod looked up at the window and scowled. Then he took a deep breath, released it, and forced a smile.

'Dad?'

'Nothing, Steve. I didn't mean to yell like that. You just gave me a fright.'

'Are you sure you're all right?'

'Yes, yes. Fine. I'm going to have a shower and get dressed. We've got a lot of work to do today. Don't be too long.'

'Just a quick dip. I'll be out in a minute.'

Rod headed back inside, refusing the urge to look at the window.

#

Steve's best mate, James, arrived at five that evening. He was a rugby player and always trained hard, but come evening, he liked to party just as hard. With his physique, he had the potential to go far in the game, but he lacked the discipline required. At any rate, he wasn't planning on making an attempt at going professional. His real passion was finance. He was a good friend, the kind you could rely on when you found yourself in a spot of bother. Rod trusted him too. He was the only one of Steve's friends who knew the code to the door.

'Looking good!' he yelled as he strode through the living room and onto the deck.

'Hey, James! Did you win?' Rod asked.

'Of course, dad,' Steve cut in, looking at his mate for confirmation.

James grinned confidently and raised his shoulders and palms to the sky.

'Good lad! One more reason to celebrate tonight.'

'Rod, you must be the coolest father in the galaxy,' James congratulated him.

'In the universe, my boy. When the old ball and chain isn't around at any rate.'

James knew all too well that it wasn't exactly Saint Valentine's every day in the Weldon household. There wasn't much he didn't know about the family. He and Steve had grown up together. Rod knew James' folks too. It wasn't all roses in their garden either.'

'It looks great here. I reckon we're set for the most legendary pool party in human history!'

'That's the plan,' Steve said.

James admired the setup. The sound system was all hooked up and there was a raised platform for the disc jockey. At the end near the garage and entrance to the living room, there were three long tables with at least a hundred plastic cocktail glasses lined up. There were twenty deck chairs around the pool, each with a brand new towel featuring sea motifs; shells, anchors, helms, turtles. At the bottom of the pool, there were imitation crabs and sea stars, and there were six plastic bottles that looked just like glass ones bobbing in the water. Each bottle was corked and contained a pencil and a piece of paper so that guests could write messages to each other.

'How did your cocktails come out?'

'They came out awesome, if I do say so myself. I've made three kinds: Sea Breeze for the princesses, Deep Blue for the ladyboys, and, for the real men, a double-strength concoction of Blackbeard's Ghost.'

James nodded his approval.

'Did you have enough time to buy The Kraken?'

'Five bottles of the spicy stuff.'

'Good one, mate. How about we get our costumes on and do a taste test?'

'Didn't you want me to help you out first?'

'It's all done. You can give me a hand pouring the drinks later, and then I'll need a sidekick for the party games I told you about. For now, I'm going to need help with my zombie pirate outfit. Are you all set?'

'Yeah, I managed to get the walrus costume I was telling you about. It's crazy, man. Don't tell anybody who's inside it though.'

'That'll be a laugh. Give me a hand with mine first, while you still have hands instead of flippers or whatever they are.'

#

By the time the guests started to roll up, Rod, Steve, and James had transformed themselves into a deep-sea diver, a zombie pirate, and a walrus, all well on the way to inebriation. The security camera showed another zombie pirate at the gate. That was Zach, a good mate of both Steve and James. The undead marauder lurched convincingly through the living room, making the three sea creatures in his wake laugh hysterically.

The pink octopus with Japanese eyes was Steve's girl, Yumi. They had met at a university party over a line of coke. Her parents, back home in Chiba, were working hard to pay for her studies and would have been deeply ashamed to know that their daughter had a secret boyfriend and was developing a drug habit. Steve grabbed her and picked her up, sticking his rotten hands up between her tentacles and her legs.

A couple of lobsters were in hot pursuit of Yumi. Their costumes were perfect, with red mesh covering their eyes and a flap over their mouths. Steve had no idea who they were, but that didn't bother him. The mystery was all part of the fun.

Darkness fell quickly. Rod switched the lights on and got the music pumping. After a few cocktails, he forgot all about the window. He even forgot about Oscar. He mingled with all of Steve's friends for a while, but once his secretary, Anastasia, got there, he stuck to her like glue.

Dave and Tim from down the street arrived next. Rod didn't especially like them, mostly just because he didn't like gays, but they always had a good supply on them. They were dressed as mermen. Their tanned, well-defined torsos were bare, and they wore blue and green sequin trousers with flared bottoms that looked just like billowing fishtails. Each had a length of rope with a closed shell around the neck, and Rod guessed that they contained not pearls, but white treasure of another kind. He made a mental note to take them aside and ask them for a snort later.

Jezza, a handsome lifesaver wearing nothing but red and yellow budgie smugglers and a swimming cap, turned up next. He was accompanied by two pretty mermaids, Cara and Amanda. They had met Jezza and Steve at another party and had accepted the invitation to come to this one, even though they barely knew the boys. Jezza, on the other hand, felt right at home. The fact that there wasn't a soul in the pool didn't stop him from blowing his whistle and shouting, 'Everybody out of the water!'

His dramatic entrance was appreciated. Everyone cheered and Steve tackled him into the pool. The party had officially kicked off.

Yumi grabbed a couple of drinks and joined the boys in the pool. Her pink tentacles slithered around her in the water. Others followed suit until the pool was teeming with strange creatures swilling cocktails and trying to move to the beat of the music.

Zach was the first to pluck one of the bottles up and write a message on it. As he wrote, he kept glancing at Cara, and once he had finished, he swam underwater and released it as he passed her. The bottle popped up right in front of her, almost between her breasts. She let out a little squeal and vainly tried to spot the messenger, before pulling the message out. She grinned cheekily as she read it.

Nothing escaped Oscar's attention as he stood at the bedroom window and peered through the curtains. He studied the dynamics of the party, watching the shenanigans intensify with every passing minute, and wondered whether the witch would make an appearance with so many witnesses, and, if so, to what end.

Steve distributed something too small for Oscar to see to the other zombie pirate and the lifesaver, while the walrus went to fetch a fourth round of cocktails. The deep-sea diver and his penguin followed the mermen inside the house, and Oscar frowned to himself. Meanwhile, the lobsters were rubbing up against each other in the pool, trying to get as close to each other as their exoskeletons would permit, and this was making the pink octopus and the two mermaids giggle.

A few minutes later, the deep-sea diver and his crew emerged from the house, and the second zombie pirate drained his cocktail and dived into the pool. He came up next to the mermaid he had sent a message to earlier. They swam to the pool stairs, got out, and hurried inside.

Nobody was acting sensibly, but nobody was acting suspiciously either. Oscar remained as still as he could and observed with practised patience. He was dressed in black jeans, a thin jumper, trainers, and gloves. The rest of his costume was on the bed, ready to be rapidly donned. For the moment, however, he was intent on gleaning whatever information he could from his discrete vantage point.

It was eleven o'clock and everybody was in the water when it happened.

'Look at the window!' someone yelled.

The witch was standing at the window with soft red light

illuminating her naked body. She was oiling her breasts, making them glow under the red light.

Oscar turned his attention back to the pool to find that it had been transformed into a huge bubble bath. He counted the heads bobbing in the foam, staring at the window—some were laughing, others were cheering, and a few were frozen in wide-mouthed wonder. The deep-sea diver's face was hidden by his helmet.

'Two missing!' he whispered to himself. Then one of them resurfaced, but it wasn't Steve.

There was no time to lose. Without another glance at the witch window, Oscar grabbed his diving mask and rushed down to the pool.

'Steve's underwater!' he shouted.

He was met with a wall of perplexed faces, but there was no time to explain.

He dived in.

It was dark in the water and Oscar couldn't see much apart from kicking legs at first. He was still trying to find his bearings when he saw Zach pulling his friend to the surface. He resurfaced immediately and helped haul Steve to the pool stairs.

Girls were screaming and Rod had taken his helmet off by then. Confusion was written all over his face. Everyone stayed back as Zach tried to resuscitate his friend.

'Call an ambulance!' Oscar shouted.

'I'm on it!' a voice called back.

'Is he going to make it?' another voice asked.

'He's not responding,' Zach replied.

The screaming and gasping grew louder.

'What was he on?'

'We're in deep shit if the cops come.'

'Why would the cops come? It was just an accident.'

Oscar had failed to predict the outcome, but he wasn't prepared to make any more mistakes. Ignoring the hysterics and the banter, he scanned the area. There was no longer any sign of the murderer. Even though it was too late to prevent the witch's attack, it wasn't yet too late to catch the culprits.

8.

Oscar dashed into the house and down the internal stairs. He ran to where the indistinct track leading through the trees began. Behind him, up on the terrace, was a world of bright lights and distraught voices. In front of him, all was dark and quiet, with only the faint glow of a street lamp below promising an issue from the brooding obscurity.

Remembering the trouble the track had given him the last time he'd taken it, and considering the fact he could barely distinguish his bare feet from the rough ground, he decided against running. Instead, he held his hands up as buffers against unseen branches and strode into the thicket as quickly as reason dictated.

As he reached the end of the track and swung himself over the boundary fence, the familiar sound of the Ford Fiesta's engine coming to life reached his ears. The car roared ambitiously, before speeding along the street. No sooner had it disappeared than the engine of a parked car turned over.

As Oscar clambered down to the footpath, the headlights flashed on and the passenger door swung open. He climbed in, and before he'd even closed the door, the car pulled out, tyres screeching.

'Edgar, as reliable as always, my friend.'

The driver made no reply as he accelerated along the street.

'I'm afraid we have a murderer on our hands,' Oscar announced despondently.

'A murderer, not merely a witch?'

'So it seems. Unless a miracle is being performed as we speak.'

Edgar turned right and stared intently ahead as he drove.

'I've lost track of them.'

'Don't panic. Keep driving along this road.'

They caught sight of two red tail lights for a moment and glimpsed the sweep of headlights as the car turned left.

'I think they're heading for Toowong Cemetery.'

Edgar offered him a quick look of surprise, before turning his attention back to the road.

'It doesn't make sense to commit murder and then escape to a cemetery.'

'It makes perfect sense,' Oscar argued. 'Where could one be more isolated and safe from witnesses? The very fact that the notion astounds you goes to show how clever it is.'

Edgar wasn't sure whether to take that personally.

'That said, I'd wager it's not practicality that sends them there, but sentimentality. I think I finally know what this is all about, Edgar.'

'Why in the world would sentimentality drive anybody to head for a cemetery after committing murder?'

'For the same reason anybody would go to a cemetery under normal circumstances.'

Edgar shook his head, keeping his eyes on the road.

'To commune with the dead.'

'Assuming you're right—and that is, of course, what I assume—I'll never know how you do it, will I?'

Oscar smiled unconvincingly.

'Offer me no praise tonight, my friend, I beg of you.

Catching a killer is a distant second to preventing a murder.'

Edgar turned left onto Birdwood Terrace, the long street forming the upper boundary of the cemetery. Silent houses slept on the left, and a line of trees and bushes to the right demarcated the cemetery, which covered the hillside sweeping down to Mount Coot-tha Road.

'There it is,' Oscar announced calmly, pointing to a patch of blue panelling peeping out from behind a hibiscus shrub.

Edgar parked the car and immediately cut the engine.

'Am I to assume we're not calling the boys in blue?'

'You are,' Oscar replied. An instant later, he decided he owed his friend at least a preliminary explanation. 'Now that we know where they are, there's no need to rush. If we go about this the right way, all will be revealed, right here, tonight. I'm convinced the evidence in this case is as weak as the motive is strong. The absurdity of the whole affair, and the nature of the party itself, makes it highly unlikely that a criminal investigation would even be opened, let alone a conviction against these atypical felons secured. This is the brilliance of their scheme.'

'Is that admiration I detect?'

'In a way, it is,' Oscar said darkly. 'At this moment, Steve's drowning is being treated as a tragic accident, the result of a deadly cocktail of drink and drugs. Of course, Mr Weldon will know that there is much more to it, and he will be expecting me to bring a glimmer of light, however transitory, to provide some meagre relief from the perpetuity of profound grief that awaits him.'

Edgar stared across the street to where ghost gums stood sentinel along the edge of the cemetery. Their white trunks and limbs reached for the sky, where dark clouds were drifting across an ashen moon.

'What are we doing here, Oscar? If justice can't be served, you have no more to do with it all.'

'That's not how I see it, Edgar. I was engaged to solve a mystery, and that's precisely what I'm doing. This turn of events only makes the need for closure all the more urgent. Are you ready to go?'

Edgar nodded. 'I'm ready.'

They got out of the car and pressed the doors closed as softly as possible. Oscar dashed across the street and into the cemetery, and Edgar followed. The moonlight provided sufficient visibility for them to see two blonde heads not far below. They weaved their way down the hill, along the narrow alleys between graves. Whenever a cloud obstructed the moon, the light would falter and shift briefly, giving the cemetery an eerie atmosphere of spectral animation. Oscar choreographed his movement with the fluctuating light, moving slightly more quickly when a dense cloud passed overhead, or when hidden in darkness or behind tall headstones or trees, and almost freezing like one of the stone angels or crosses when exposed by direct moonlight. Edgar quickly understood what he was doing and followed his example.

Oscar stopped by a headstone so precariously slanted it would make the Leaning Tower of Pisa envious, turned to Edgar, and raised a finger to his lips, even though he'd been as stealthy as an owl. He then indicated that he would go right and Edgar would approach from the left.

Edgar gave him a thumbs-up.

The two young women were sitting on the slab of a well-maintained grave, with a vase containing fresh flowers between them and the headstone. Oscar spoke before he and Edgar closed in on them. After all, regardless of the circumstances, two men confronting two women in a cemetery in the middle of the night called for a certain degree of tact.

'Good evening, ladies. Please don't panic. We just want to talk to you for a moment.'

Of course, even the polite words and friendly tone didn't cut it. They turned with a start and got to their feet. Their eyes were wide, but more with alarm than fear.

Oscar and Edgar stopped their two-pronged advance, halting two plots away.

'Sit down, I beg of you. We need to have a little chat together.'

They remained standing.

'My name is Oscar Tremont, and this is my associate, Edgar Douglas.'

'You're not with the police?'

'We are not. Would you rather talk to the police?' Oscar asked, raising his eyebrows.

The women looked at each and decided to resume their places.

Oscar came closer and crouched beside the grave. Edgar remained where he was.

The young women were wearing tracksuits now, but Oscar recognised them all the same. One of them had hair that was still quite wet, and the other smelled of the essential oils she had rubbed over her breasts.

'A mermaid and a witch,' Oscar mused.

'What are talking about?' Amanda asked, shaking her head.

'You'll never win an Oscar if that's your idea of acting. On the other hand, your sister plays the witch very well. That performance has certainly changed the stereotype of the old crone I've always imagined.'

She couldn't suppress a fleeting smile, but it was full of sadness.

'You don't know that we're sisters,' Amanda replied.
'I do. But your real name probably isn't Amanda,' he said.
They remained stone-faced.
'You were at the party? I didn't notice you.'
'There are three names engraved on the headstone,' Oscar continued, indicating them respectfully with upraised palms. 'The most recent one is Dana Frazer. She was your sister. Do you have a photograph of her in the seashell around your neck?'
She stared at him, wide-eyed.
'How did you know?'
'In your place, that's exactly what I would keep in it.'
She unzipped her top and pulled the seashell from her cleavage.
'Would you like to see?'
'I would, if you don't mind.'
'You shouldn't, Kirsten.'
'Ah, Kirsten,' Oscar repeated. 'And you are?'
'I'm Isabel,' she admitted with a sigh.
'I want him to know who she was,' Kirsten said. 'There's nothing wrong with us visiting the grave of our sister.'
She opened the shell and showed Oscar the portrait of Dana. It was the photograph of a happy girl, ignorant of the tragedy that awaited her.
'What else did your shell contain earlier this evening?' Oscar asked.
'Nothing,' Kirsten answered stolidly. 'What are you insinuating?'
'You asked if we were policemen. Why?'
'We come to visit our sister at night, and every now and then, the police tell us to leave. You're not supposed to come here afterhours.'

'Aren't those officers usually constables in uniform?'
'Usually.'
'You're private investigators?' Isabel asked.
'That's correct.'
'You seem to know a lot about us, but why are you investigating us? We're not vandals. Nobody respects this place more than us.'
'It just seems strange that you left the party so quickly after the accident.'
'Accident?' Kirsten asked. 'Everything was fine when I left the party.'
'I wasn't even there. I just picked my sister up.'
Their acting was improving by the minute. Oscar was genuinely impressed.
'You don't know about the drowning?'
They gasped.
'Who drowned?'
'Steve,' Oscar said, studying their faces.
'Is he...?' Isabel asked.
'Yes, he is.'
'That's dreadful,' Kirsten said, almost convincingly.
'Your sister drowned, didn't she?'
'She did,' Kirsten confirmed, keeping her voice as even as possible. 'She drowned at Tallebudgera Beach after a wild party. She was mixed up with a bad crowd and taking drugs.'
The final piece of the puzzle fell into place.
'Can I tell you what I think?'
The sisters looked at each other in silent consultation.
'I'm curious,' Kirsten said.
'Dana and Steve were an item, and your sister was into the parties and the drugs for a while, but she soon grew tired of all that. She'd decided to call it off. I believe your sister told Steve

it was over the night she drowned.'

The tears on their cheeks glistened in the moonlight, and Oscar knew they were heartfelt. There were no theatrics in their grief.

'You can understand why I'm suspicious about your movements tonight?'

'I suppose we can,' Kirsten admitted. 'It's understandable, isn't it, Isabel?'

'I guess so, but what happened tonight has nothing to do with us. It was surely just an accident.'

'Fate, one might say,' Kirsten said.

'The police might launch an investigation if they find evidence of foul play. It could be that fate had a helping hand.'

'They might,' Kirsten said, wiping her tears away. 'But the coroner will probably rule that the death was the result of a mountain of drugs and an ocean of alcohol in combination with dangerous poolside antics. I hardly think they'll come to the conclusion that witchcraft was involved. This isn't the sixteenth century after all.'

Isabel placed a finger on the headstone and traced the engraved name of their dearly missed sister.

'I'm sorry for your loss,' Oscar whispered, getting to his feet. He glanced up at the moon and closed his eyes for a moment.

Kirsten and Isabel held each other tight as they watched the two men walk away.

Epilogue

Two days later, Oscar joined Edgar at his house. He brought a bottle of scotch with him. They both needed a stiff drink, and Oscar owed his friend an explanation.

'He knew about Dana Frazer?'

'He knew Steve had something to hide. I suppose the witch business seemed so bizarre to him he never even thought there could be a connection. He'd assumed he was the target.'

'If he'd told you, his son might still be alive today.'

Oscar sipped his whisky and stared through the glass, deep in thought.

'What happens now?' Edgar asked.

'Nothing at all. Case closed. He's paid me my fee, and even added a bonus, which I hardly deserve. He's convinced, or wants me to believe he's convinced, it was all a prank gone wrong.'

'He wants to avoid a scandal,' Edgar grumbled.

'Precisely.'

'I suppose we all have our secrets to keep.'

'That we do,' Oscar agreed. 'In the hearts of men are kept secrets darker than the deepest seas.'

Edgar sipped his whisky thoughtfully. 'Who said that?' he asked after a moment.

'What's that, Edgar?'

'The line you just quoted.'

Oscar shot his friend a moustache-twitching grin.

'I shouldn't have asked.' Edgar laughed. 'You're also a poet of the strange and inexplicable now, are you?'

The Secret of the Severed Hand

Oscar Tremont waited for the boiling water to cool down just a little before pouring it into the porcelain teapot. He watched the dried herbs leap and pirouette in the strainer. Every time he made herbal tea, the choreography was familiar yet slightly different, like a game of chess with Edgar Douglas. Once the performance had come to a close, he put the lid on the teapot and took his favourite cup—the one with a blue dragon weaving its way through wispy clouds—from the corner shelf that overlooked the kitchen sink. He carried the pot and cup back to the verandah and placed them on the antique tea trolley before lowering himself onto his thinking chair. Then, closing his eyes, he listened to the heavy summer downpour as it made the tin roof of his cottage sing a discordant but mesmerising tune.

A minute later, a crash of thunder shook the earth, acting as the cymbal in the celestial orchestra.

Oscar opened his eyes and poured himself a cup of tea, then closed them again and drew a deep breath.

Another crash of thunder shook the earth. It seemed to have come from directly above Dover Street. His cottage shuddered and the neighbourhood dogs unleashed a barrage of nervous barks.

He loved thunderstorms as much as Louise hated them. This particular storm wouldn't be bothering her though. She was at Chermside Shopping Centre, protected from the weather by three levels of shops, food courts, and cinemas—all encased in a monstrous concrete box.

A gust of wind blew rain onto the verandah, sprinkling his bare feet, while the warm tea tantalised his tongue with the taste of mint, lemon, and hibiscus. He perceived a powerful flash of light through his closed eyelids and braced himself for the clap of thunder. It came a fraction of a second later, and for an instant, he thought his house would come tumbling down around him.

Then, as the rumbling of the angry sky subsided, another sound reached his ears. It was the creaking of the gate to his front garden. He had a visitor, despite the wild weather. A client? He certainly needed more business.

Oscar opened his eyes.

The elderly man seemed insignificant under his enormous black and red umbrella. Water was cascading off it at eight equally spaced points, making it seem as though he were imprisoned in a cage of crystal bars. He closed the gate behind him and looked over to the verandah.

'Please, come in out of the rain,' Oscar urged him, sitting up.

The man wasted no time in weaving his way around a few puddles and climbing the stairs to the verandah. An expression of distress and helplessness covered a venerable face that Oscar sensed was more used to portraying gravitas and calm. This was an elderly gentleman who had seen much of the world and lived through challenging times. His demeanour, despite its present state of dismay, spoke as loudly and clearly as words ever could.

Oscar got to his feet and pulled a canvas chair up for his visitor. The man was slim but certainly not frail. His body still retained signs of strength. His rolled-up sleeves exposed sinewy forearms.

'Please, take a seat.'

He lowered himself gracefully onto the chair. His movements and deportment denied what his face suggested.

'You are Oscar Tremont? I have come to the right address?'

Oscar nodded slowly. 'Yes, I am, and, yes, I believe you have indeed. An inexplicable turn of events has disturbed your routine and shown you that you are not in control as much as you would like to think. You are a man who is accustomed to resolving problems with a cool head and a strong will. You have faced challenges before, probably far more menacing than the one which now confronts you, but the present situation defies explanation and has made you question what you know about yourself and the world you inhabit. You hesitated before coming here to seek my assistance, but upon deciding you had no other option, you came as quickly as you could.'

'Good,' he said. 'I see I've come to the right place. You seem to know everything about me already. I don't know whether I should be comforted or disturbed by that.'

'On the contrary,' Oscar humbly replied. 'I know very little about you. For example, I don't know your name.'

The man raised his right hand to his chest in apology. Oscar's attention was drawn to the signet ring on his little finger, but he didn't get a good look at the design it bore.

'My name is Charles Lethbridge and I have a problem the likes of which I have never had before.' A flash of lightning made him jump. Then an almighty clap of thunder mocked him. He looked out into the rain and shivered. 'A problem the likes of which you would not believe. I'm afraid you will think me senile.'

Oscar shook his head, dismissing the man's fear.

'I'd rather be dead than taken for a batty old fool.'

'It is clear to me that you are far from being batty or foolish, Mister Lethbridge. I have been given the task of solving numerous mysteries that defy conventional wisdom and they have all stemmed from very real causes. Behind every ghost and ghoul is the dark heart of a flesh-and-blood human being. Please, tell me exactly why you have come here so I can tackle the problem quickly and effectively.'

'Very well, but it may take some time.'

'That's perfectly all right. The more you can tell me, the better I can serve you. Perhaps you would like a cup of tea?'

Charles Lethbridge gripped the arms of his canvas chair and pulled himself closer to Oscar Tremont. He wanted to whisper something, even though the two of them were alone and the noise of the storm made eavesdropping impossible.

'I do apologise for being so forward, but I'm rather shaken up, as you can tell. You wouldn't happen to have something stronger, would you?'

Oscar winked, then jumped up and went inside to grab a bottle of Talisker Storm and two glasses.

The men sipped at their whiskies and felt the warmth spread throughout their bodies as the rain and the wind continued to rage beyond the verandah.

'This is a remarkable tale, Mister Tremont. So, before I begin, I must ask that you will not dismiss it as the ravings of a deranged old man.'

'I have told you, Mister Lethbridge, that I am sure you have a keen and reasonable mind. Do not worry about my thoughts. Just make sure you tell me as much as you can about this affair.'

Charles nodded, took another sip of scotch, and drew a deep breath.

'Are you familiar with the works of the French writer, Guy de Maupassant?'

Oscar smiled. 'I most certainly am. My wife is French and I speak her mother tongue fluently. I have read most of Guy de Maupassant's tales in the original French.'

Charles was clearly impressed.

'In that case, you know the story of the severed hand?'

'*La Main.* I certainly do. It's a classic tale of supernatural horror.'

'That it is. What if I told you that it was not simply a work of fiction but a true story?'

Oscar looked at the man blankly. He had promised to keep an open mind and he wasn't about to break that promise or risk offending his client.

'Please continue.'

'Well, it all started about twenty years ago, when I was in Normandy. I was visiting the scene of the landing that claimed my two older brothers at Sword Beach. I was with my wife—may she rest in peace—and after the pilgrimage to the D-Day beaches, we spent a few days relaxing in the seaside town of Etretat. During our time there, we went to an auction and bought several rather unusual souvenirs. I must tell you that I have always, much to my wife's regret, been attracted to bizarre relics. I have a collection that you simply have to see to believe. But unfortunately, my finest exhibit is now missing.'

'The severed hand?'

Charles smiled faintly. 'That's right, Mister Tremont. The severed hand that I bought in Etretat and that was locked away securely in a glass display cabinet has escaped.'

Escaped. The choice of word struck Oscar as peculiar, but he didn't voice his thoughts. He had other questions to ask first.

'Mister Lethbridge, can you tell me about the person who sold you the severed hand?'

'I'm sorry but I can't really. It was, after all, twenty years ago, and I have had no contact with the *brocanteur* since then. I don't think I even asked him his name.'

'He told you that the severed hand was really the hand of the criminal in Guy de Maupassant's tale?'

'Yes.' Charles Lethbridge laughed, looking Oscar in the eye, trying to read the mind of the Investigator of the Strange and Inexplicable. 'Of course, I didn't believe a word of it. I didn't believe in ghosts, and I certainly didn't believe that a human hand severed centuries ago could really scurry around like an enormous arachnid. I just bought it because it clearly *was* the severed hand of a human being and therefore qualifies as a bizarre relic.'

'It certainly does,' Oscar agreed. 'So, what precisely happened?'

'A few days ago—it must have been Monday evening—I noticed it had moved. I seldom remove it from its display cabinet, and when I do, I always put it back carefully, placing it on a small red cushion. I lock the cabinet and keep the key hidden. You can imagine how I felt when I saw the hand leaning against the glass, its fingertips pressed against the pane as though it were some grotesque spider seeking a way out of its vivarium!'

'That must have been terribly frightening indeed.'

'You can say that again! I thought I'd lost my mind. I went to check that the key to the cabinet was where I always kept it, and it was.'

'Had anyone been in the house around that time?'

'Just my son, but he wouldn't play a trick like that on me. And there was no sign anyone had broken in.'

'I see,' Oscar said. 'A short time later, the hand *escaped*?'

'Precisely. I know it sounds ridiculous, but that's exactly what happened. It was the day before yesterday, I came home from town around ten o'clock at night. I'd had a few drinks, but nothing that would cause hallucinations. I unlocked the door to my house and went inside. I'm a fairly observant sort of fellow and usually notice if anything is out of place. Nothing was. I went to my study, where I keep my exhibits, and was going to read a little before going to bed when I saw that the display cabinet that housed the severed hand was lying on the ground, as though it had fallen over. The glass had been smashed, presumably as a result of the fall, and the severed hand was missing.'

'The day before yesterday was Wednesday, and so today is Friday,' Oscar pointed out.

'That's right,' Charles confirmed.

'It sounds as though someone who knew you had the hand and wanted it desperately has been playing games with you. This person entered your house on at least two occasions and wants you to think that the hand has somehow become reanimated, like in Guy de Maupassant's tale. You suspect that the hand knocked the cabinet over in a desperate attempt to escape but it is surely more likely that it was pulled over by the thief.'

'I'd like to think you're right, Mister Tremont. It would calm my nerves. For some reason, as unreal as it may sound, I can't help but think it's more likely the hand escaped than that somebody managed to enter my house without leaving a trace and stole it, taking nothing else.'

Oscar drained his glass, put it down slowly, and consulted his silver pocket watch.

'I'd like to investigate the scene.'

'Good. I knew I'd come to the right man. I simply couldn't have gone to the police with such a fantastic case.'

'Quite out of the question,' Oscar agreed. 'That, surely, was the whole point of the elaborate set-up. If we are to rule out the supernatural and accept that you have become the victim of a professional thief, as I insist we should, the only rational explanation for this *mise-en-scène* is to either convince you no crime has been committed by human hands or make you feel too embarrassed to go to the police.'

'It certainly worked. I almost didn't come to you either.'

'But you did, and that may turn out to be the perpetrator's only miscalculation. I won't know until I've studied the scene. That said, I have a feeling a second mistake is about to be made.'

'What do you mean by that?'

'Judging by the nature of the crime, I'd say we're dealing with someone who craves order and method, and people like that tend to follow patterns. Monday—Wednesday—'

'Friday. Today! You think there'll be a third act?'

'It's just a hunch. I take it you usually go out on Monday, Wednesday, and Friday evenings and stay home the rest of the week?'

'That's right. I'm rather predictable, I'm afraid.'

'You can tell me more about that later. We'll have plenty of time this evening. Would it be terribly inconvenient if I stayed the night with you? If I'm right, we may just catch a thief, and if you're right, I might save you from being strangled in your sleep by the severed hand.'

Charles Lethbridge stared at Oscar wide-eyed and it was several seconds before he could manage to reply, 'No, my good man. No inconvenience whatsoever.'

#

His house was a fifteen-minute walk from Dover Street. The thunderstorm had passed and the streets now sparkled. But evening would soon descend on Brisbane, depriving the sun of the opportunity to turn the streets into a sauna.

'Has anyone ever expressed interest in the severed hand as far as you can remember?' Oscar asked.

'Well, I don't show it to just anyone, and I'm not in the habit of inviting large numbers of people to my home or hosting dinner parties. To be honest, I can't think of a soul who has ever shown a desire to possess it. Most of those who have seen it were simultaneously intrigued and disgusted. No-one has ever even asked me for the privilege of holding it. They all seemed happy to let it remain in its glass cabinet. I really can't think who would have even entertained the idea of stealing it.'

'No obvious suspects,' Oscar said. 'Another question; prior to Monday evening, when you saw the hand pressed against the glass as though trying to escape, had you ever spoken to anyone at all about your belief that the hand might be able to move of its own accord.'

He smiled and shook his head. 'No, I told those who saw the hand about its supposed history, that I had been told by the *brocanteur* that it was the hand behind Guy de Maupassant's famous tale, but none of them seemed particularly impressed and many didn't even know who Maupassant was. For my part, I'd never entertained the idea that the hand might be able to move until I saw it had changed position inside the cabinet.'

'And it seemed that the key hadn't been removed.'

'That's right. It was hidden where I always keep it.'

Oscar nodded. The question of how the hand had moved would be the first he would need to answer.

'Here we are. This is my house.'

They stopped between a silver Mazda sedan parked at the kerb and a grand Queenslander that stood well off the ground on solid stumps. A verandah skirted the house on the front and one side, and a broad staircase with hibiscus bushes growing on either side provided access to the latticework door.

'You have a beautiful home, Mister Lethbridge.'

'Thank you. This is where I grew up. My brother and I lived here for many years, until he moved down south. Then I got married and started a family, still living here. Now I live here alone. I know it's a big house for one man, but I don't want to leave it after all these years.'

'You certainly look after it.'

'I do what I can. My son is a great help, I must admit. Neither of us are real handymen, but we manage.'

Oscar scanned the house, examining the various points of access. As they walked up the stairs, he studied the treads, the railings, and the door Charles was about to unlock. Nothing was disturbed. There were no signs of a break-in, just as Charles had told him.

'Follow me, I'll show you where the hand should be. I haven't touched the scene of the crime, if that's what it was.'

As they walked down the hallway, Charles removed an old mortice key from his pocket. He stopped at a door, inserted the key into the keyhole, turned it, and pushed the door open.

Oscar found himself in a veritable cabinet of curiosities. It was the kind of room he would have loved to have in his house, and he realised that if he were a burglar, such a treasure trove would be at the top of his list of targets. There was an eclectic mix of the unusual and exotic from all around the globe. There were tribal masks from the jungles of New Guinea and bundles of carved spears. There was a Japanese katana in its ornate sheath and a Spanish rapier and jewel-encrusted Mughal dagger fixed to the wall. He spotted an antique harpoon and net with stone weights, presumably of Scandinavian origin, and an Amazonian shrunken head appeared to be deep in conversation with a crocodile skull. A mediaeval thumbscrew sat innocently on a bench next to a chastity belt, and a gong and mallet hid underneath.

The room was another world where the bizarre and the frightening were normal.

'You have a truly amazing collection!'

Charles nodded proudly, but he was looking towards the far corner of the room, where a broken glass cabinet lay on the floor.

Oscar walked over to the cabinet as slowly as a pallbearer, except that his eyes were not fixed straight ahead, but were darting around, studying everything. He knelt by the cabinet and stared at its broken pane, as though expecting to find an answer there.

'The cabinet was locked the first time you saw the hand had moved?'

'Yes, yes,' Charles said.

'I want you to do me a favour. I want you to find something, not too fragile, that is about the same size and weight as the hand.'

Charles frowned. He didn't understand why Oscar would make such a request, but he knew the man he had gone to for help was the greatest private investigator in town, if not the entire country.

Oscar lifted the cabinet, careful not to cut himself on the jagged shards of glass.

'Will this do?' He had found what looked like a child's doll, but the pins sticking out of its back and limbs told otherwise.

'It's perfect.'

Oscar took the voodoo doll and placed it on the red cushion in the centre of the shelf. He then turned the cabinet around so that a pane that had not been smashed in the fall faced them. He grasped the top of the cabinet and tilted it towards himself. The little red cushion remained in the centre, but the voodoo doll toppled down until its movement was blocked by the pane of glass. Oscar then let the cabinet tip back to its normal position, standing vertically. The voodoo doll remained leaning against the glass.

'Oh, now I understand!' Charles exclaimed.

'So, this is more or less how you found the severed hand the day you saw it had been moved?'

'Yes, it is. How simple it must have been for someone to do that! Quite stupid of me!'

'No, my good fellow. You mustn't say that. Not stupid. Unimaginative at worst.'

'This means an intruder came in here and did what you just did, and then came back Wednesday evening to steal the hand. For some reason, I find that thought more disturbing than that of the hand moving of its own accord.'

'As do I,' Oscar agreed solemnly, looking around the room. A bookshelf holding dozens of leather-bound volumes caught his eye. He strolled over to it, navigating his way around a magnificent celestial globe. 'You have some fine old books here. Extremely valuable ones. This original 1885 copy of Maupassant's *Contes du jour et de la nuit* is a veritable treasure.'

'It's the pride of my collection,' Charles admitted proudly.

Oscar carefully slid the book from its place and looked at the gap now left between *Bel-Ami* and *Le Horla*. When he turned to Charles, disappointment was written on his face.

'Oh, what a surprise! It looks like I've stumbled across the cabinet key's hidey-hole.'

'I thought it was a clever place to hide it,' Charles said sheepishly.

'We have one unfortunate trait, cultivated men like us.'

'We fall into the trap of underestimating others?'

Oscar nodded. 'To be honest, almost anywhere else in the room would have been a better hiding place. I suspect you were too clever for your own good.'

'You keep the key to this room on your person?'

'Always.'

'Who else has a copy of it?'

'Only my son.'

Oscar studied the door and its lock. 'I could easily pick it,' he mused. 'The front door is a different matter. On the other hand, gaining access to the verandah without using the door would present no great challenge to an agile burglar.'

Charles watched Oscar as he walked over to the room's sole window, which opened onto the verandah. The window was of a kind common in old Queenslanders; the lower pane opened by sliding up and locked in place with a simple metal clasp, while the upper pane was fixed in the frame. Outside access was generally prevented by leaning an upright length of wood or metal on top of the lower pane frame so that it would jam if one tried to slide the window up.

'Stand here by the window, please.'

Charles followed the instruction and Oscar left the room. A moment later he appeared on the verandah, on the other side of the window. He slid the tips of his fingers between the sill and the bottom edge of the frame.

'I'm going to push up to try to open the window,' he told Charles through the pane.

Charles shrugged, glancing up at the metal rod on top of the lower pane frame.

Oscar pushed quickly, jamming the rod, and the window jarred. The gap was too narrow to even allow his fingers under.

'No way of getting in through the window,' Charles told him, shaking his head.

'Not so fast. It just requires a gentler approach.'

Oscar lowered the window until the frame pressed his fingertips against the sill. He then jiggled the frame up and down, making it vibrate, and Charles frowned as the bottom of the metal rod slid further along the top of the frame. Once the rod lay flat, Oscar pushed the window all the way up.

'I'm sorry, but it's just that easy,' he told Charles as he flipped the clasp into place to hold the window open and climbed into the room.

Charles frowned. 'But the window was closed.'

'No problem.' Oscar undid the clasp, and holding the window frame steady with one hand, he slid the metal rod back to a diagonal position with the other. Once he'd wiggled himself back through the opening, he slid the window down ever so slowly until it was closed.

Charles stared at him, blank-faced, through the window.

'That, my dear fellow, is how it was done,' Oscar said, as he came back into the room.

'I think I'm beginning to get into the thief's head,' Charles mused. 'Unable to open the door to the room, and being forced to both come and go by climbing the verandah and sneaking through the window, the thief couldn't steal much at once. Realising this, he thought up this ruse to give me the spooks, knowing that I'd feel too foolish to go to the police. As a result, the way would be open to come back whenever I was out and each theft of item after item would only strengthen my belief that the hand was hiding in here, rummaging about at night.'

'You've hit the nail on the head. It's really quite ingenious, isn't it?'

Charles couldn't disagree, although he found Oscar's apparent admiration for the thief rather unsettling.

'Pretend you still suspected the hand of moving of its own accord. How would you react?'

'I don't know. I was terrified when I went to you, and I suppose that sense of dread would have worsened. I can't bear to think how I would have ended up. I don't think I could have left the house. I know I could never sell it. I guess I'd have kept this door locked, forsaking my collection and feeling the hairs on the back of my neck prick up every time I walked past.'

'That is precisely what the thief was counting on, and to my mind, that is a far worse crime than theft. You would have become a shadow of your former self, either staying here a prisoner to your unease or losing a grip on reality to the point of being admitted to an institution.'

Charles gave a slight shudder but immediately squared his shoulders and stiffened his upper lip.

'Not to worry,' Oscar chirped, then shot his client a mischievous grin. 'The battlefield has been identified, the date of the encounter announced, and the enemy's tactics revealed. We have the upper hand. You'll forgive my enthusiasm, won't you? We have two steps to take before nightfall.' He looked at Charles, eager to get him involved.

'Well, we need to set a trap?'

Oscar's mouth stretched into an enormous grin and he pumped his fist into the air. 'Yes!'

'And the second step,' he wondered. 'I'm not sure. Contact

the police?'

Oscar's eyebrows arched. 'Good grief, no! There'll be time for that later. I don't want those sods stealing my thunder. What do I want before we catch the thief? You should want it too!'

Charles stroked his chin, pondering the question, then his eyes narrowed. 'Well, you want to solve your mystery, don't you? You want to discover the identity of the thief before it's revealed to you.'

'Yes—and the only way we can do that is by talking. I'll ask you a lot of questions and you need to give me full and honest answers.'

'Understood.'

'First things first—the trap.' Oscar looked around the room. 'Perfect! We have what we need right here.'

Charles surveyed his collection of odd artefacts, wondering what the detective had in mind.

#

The trap in place, Oscar turned to his client. 'We need to sit somewhere comfortable and have a long chat. In the absence of physical clues, only your insight can reveal the culprit to me.'

'Let's sit in the living room. Anything to eat or drink?'

'Just a glass of water for the moment, please.'

Charles showed Oscar to the living room before fetching two glasses and a bottle of water from the fridge.

Oscar sat on the leather sofa and looked about the room. There were cabinets teeming with objects ranging from the busts of composers and tribal statuettes to obscure musical instruments. There was a Bolivian pan flute and a Breton *biniou kozh*. There were also several bookshelves, but the volumes here were not as rare as those kept in the study.

'Where do I start?' Charles asked, sitting in his leather armchair and pouring two glasses of water.

'Well, it's likely the thief is someone you know, or at least, someone who knows you. Whoever it is knows you keep a collection of rare and expensive objects in your home and knows you're absent three nights a week.'

'That seems likely.'

'You are the member of a club of some description?' Oscar pointed at his client's hand. 'It's a rather exclusive club and your signet ring, I would hazard, represents your adhesion to it.'

'That's very astute,' Charles said. 'But it's pure guesswork, I would hazard?'

Oscar smiled and raised his hands in surrender. Quite so—pure guesswork.'

'You're absolutely right, of course,' he said, raising the hand in question to allow Oscar to study the ring.

Amicitia Vita Est. The text was wrapped under the image of two horses raring at the start box.

'Friendship is life,' Oscar translated.

'I'm going to be terribly disappointed in you if you don't recognise it.'

'I'm not part of that illustrious set,' Oscar admitted with a wink, 'but I certainly recognise it. You're a member of Tattersalls.'

'That's right,' Charles said, not without a touch of pride.

'Being a gentlemen's club, and the country's finest, I believe, I expect your acquaintances are all men who enjoy your trust?'

'These men are my friends. I would trust them with my

life,' Charles said solemnly, leaving no doubt as to the gravity of his words.

Oscar clasped his hands together and held them to his lips. He set no store by so-called gentlemen's clubs, and suspected it was a pit of well-dressed and well-mannered snakes. All the same, if his client didn't doubt the loyalty of his friends, he was by no means going to cast aspersions.

'My friends would never do this to me. I've known them for years. We've worked together, travelled together, mourned together, and even cried on each other's shoulders.'

'Fair enough, but there has to be a link somehow. Tell me about them. Who do you talk to about your collection? How old are they? How long have you known them? Tell me about their close friends and family.'

'The members present at the club on any given night vary, but I always have a quiet drink and a cigar with the same tight circle. There are four of us. The other three are Bill Kerr, Duncan Scott, and Larry Moeller.'

'How times have changed! A Kerr and a Scott friends for life?'

Charles frowned for a moment, until the allusion dawned on him.

'Indeed! I've never thought of it before. There was a blood feud between those clans back in Scotland.'

Oscar grinned broadly. 'Well, their reiving days are long over. I'll not accuse a man of wrongdoing because of his name alone.'

'They're all around my age and in similar shape. Even if I were to suspect them for a split second, climbing up the verandah and through the window? Not a chance.'

'Would they have spoken to third parties about your collection, even quite innocently?'

'It's possible. They wouldn't have spoken to anyone they didn't trust. Just family, I should think.'

Oscar motioned for him to continue.

'Bill Kerr is much like myself. He's an old boy with quite a collection of artefacts of his own. He has a daughter and a granddaughter. Duncan is married and has a brother in Brisbane and children living in England. Larry lives alone. You could say we're his only family.'

'Tell me about Bill's daughter and granddaughter.'

'What can I say? I haven't seen them in years. What are their names? Ah, that's right, Fiona and Kelly. Fiona runs a hotel with her husband. Kelly's an only daughter, like her mother, but she's not so lucky in love. Been in and out of difficult relationships.'

'Keeps falling for the bad boys, hey?'

'Pretty much.'

Oscar looked at him and waited for a reaction.

'I don't know. No, not her.'

'Nobody could have heard the four of you talking? There must be others in the habit of sitting nearby, within earshot?'

Charles closed his eyes, visualising the lounge.

'There are two younger men who keep to themselves, playing cards mostly. They often sit in the same lounge, and possibly close enough to overhear us.'

'Do you know them?'

'Not well. They're stock brokers, I believe.'

'Indeed,' Oscar mused, his tone clearly conveying his contempt.

The smirk on his client's face told him it hadn't gone unnoticed.

'You don't know their names?'

Charles shook his head. 'I could call Larry. He'd know.'

'Please.'

Charles called his friend.

'Hello, Larry. How are you doing?' He smiled. 'No, I haven't changed my mind. Something's popped up. I'll explain later. Listen, I have a question for you.'

Oscar listened to every word Charles said, and could also hear Larry quite well. The men in question were both Brisbane Grammar boys, now working as brokers. Jason Henderson was also making a name for himself as an art dealer. He didn't know much about Evan Hodges.

'I was just wondering, that's all. I have a friend who's looking for a stock broker and had a feeling we had some contacts.' He raised his eyebrows. 'Oh, you wouldn't?' Charles bit his lip. 'I won't recommend them then. It's just that they often sit behind us at the club.' He listened and a frown formed on his brow. 'I think you're right. I didn't notice them Wednesday night. They weren't there Monday either, were they?'

Oscar leaned forward as Charles ended the conversation.

'A stock broker who deals in art on the side. Sold!' Oscar quipped. 'They're both young and fit?'

'By the look of them.'

'I wonder if they're both in on it. One to break in and the other waiting in the car, acting as lookout?'

'It's likely. Or perhaps Evan simply doesn't come to the club without Jason.'

'Also very plausible. I guess we'll soon find out.'

'I hope we're not in for any rough stuff,' Charles said.

'Rough stuff! That's a turn of phrase one doesn't hear much these days. You've been watching too many old Bogart films, haven't you?'

Charles laughed.

'Don't worry. I may not look it, but I know how to take care of myself. Let's do one last dress rehearsal before the big performance.'

'Followed by a whisky to calm the nerves?'

'You're getting the hang of this,' Oscar replied with a wink.

#

The first bump came just before ten o'clock. The house was in complete darkness and the only other sounds to be heard were the distant droning of traffic on Newmarket Road and the muffled voices coming from the television next door. Soft-soled sneakers landed on the verandah with barely more of a thud than a cat would make. Gloved hands raised the window ever so slightly, jiggling the frame just as Oscar had demonstrated, until the metal rod slid.

The burglar entered, carefully closed the window again, and switched on a torch.

A slow scan of the room revealed that all was as expected. The beam came to rest on that night's target—the jewel encrusted Mughal dagger.

It was then that a faint shuffle reached the intruder's ears, but it was too late, the net had been cast and the room's light flashed on, blinding after the darkness.

'The game's up, Mister Henderson!' Oscar growled. 'Don't try any funny business!'

The man was in his early forties, Oscar guessed, with short brown hair, neatly cut. He blinked against the light, then settled on a squint. His blue eyes fixed the detective, who gripped the net with one hand and the gong mallet with the other.

'How?' he hissed.

'It was either you or the severed hand,' Oscar replied, 'and I always bet on the intact and unmummified human, especially when he's a stock broker.'

'You're a disgrace to the club,' Charles admonished him from where he stood by the light switch.

Jason glowered at him through the net.

'You thought you'd drive me mad? You thought I'd let you help yourself to my artefacts?'

'I'm not saying a word.' Turning to Oscar, he said, 'You're not a cop. You have no right to detain me.'

'I hope you know more about making a killing out of people's savings and selling stolen goods than you do about the law. Are you familiar with Section 546 of the Criminal Code Act of 1899?'

No comment.

'Charles, perhaps it's time to call the police?'

'Wait a minute! You don't want to do that,' the detainee pleaded.

'Why ever not?' Oscar asked.

'Don't you want the severed hand?'

'The police will find it at your house.'

He grinned mischievously. 'It's already moved on. If you want it, you'll have to negotiate. No police and not a word to Tattersalls.'

'He's bluffing,' Oscar said, shaking his head.

'Is that a risk you're willing to take, Charles? Even if you call the police, you don't have any proof that I've already taken a single item from your house.'

'You got all that?' Oscar asked his client.

Charles took his smart phone from his shirt pocket and stopped the voice recorder.

'It's all here. By the way, I got a message from my son.

There's an empty Tesla parked around the corner.'

'That'll be his,' Oscar said.

'I'm not bluffing,' Jason declared. 'Is that a risk you're willing to take?'

'Justice or a severed hand?' Charles mused.

Jason squirmed like a fish out of water, but Oscar twisted his hand, tightening the net.

'It's your call, Charles, but I know what I'd choose.'

'You're absolutely right, Oscar. It's high time I let the hand roam free if that is to be its lot. I choose justice!'

Charles made the call.

For news, reviews, competitions, author interviews, and exclusive excerpts

Visit our website
blackbeaconbooks.com

Like us on Facebook
facebook.com/BlackBeaconBooks

Join us on Twitter
@BlackBeacons

Enjoy the photos on Instagram
instagram.com/blackbeaconbooks

Subscribe on Patreon
patreon.com/blackbeaconbooks

Also Available from Black Beacon Books

A short, stormy anthology designed to be read while the wind howls and the thunder booms. Batten down the hatches and take shelter!

**BLACK
BEACON
BOOKS**

blackbeaconbooks.com

Printed in Great Britain
by Amazon